The
IRONSTONE QUARRIES
of the
MIDLANDS

History, Operation and Railways

Part I
Introduction
by
Eric Tonks
M.Sc., F.R.I.C., Dip.Maths.

'*Where Iron is taken from the Earth*' Job 28.2 (New English Bible)

Book Law Publications
Nottingham

© Eric Tonks 1988

ISBN 978-1-907094-00-2

First Published in 1988
by
Runpast Publishing

This Edition Published in 2009
by
Book Law Publications

Printed by The Amadeus Press, Cleckheaton, BD19 4TQ

To Tim Barclay, who suggested a book of this kind.

An everyday scene in the ironstone quarries. A Barclay locomotive pulls away with its load on 21st August 1968 from Newton West Quarry, Storefield. Northamptonshire, while the driver of the Ransomes & Rapier 490 electric shovel examines the working face.(G. H. Starmer)

FOREWORD

There can be few industries whose life span can be so precisely determined as that of the Midlands ironstone industry, which started in 1851 and came to an end in 1980; indeed, we can almost narrow it down to the month. In the late 1950's, when 'Ironstone Railways and Tramways of the Midlands' was being written, the industry was enjoying a spell of prosperity and optimism, with plans extending well beyond the year 2000 being confidently made; the rapid decline of the succeeding quarter century—as rapid as the expansion at the beginning—could not have been foreseen. Its passing is regretted most by those whose livelihood it was; and also by a considerable body of enthusiasts—for railways in particular—who found pleasure in recording this essentially rural industry. The opportunity has been taken to tell here and in subsequent volumes the story of those 130 years.

CONTENTS

Stainby Sidings, Lincolnshire; looking north, 21st July 1963. Siding at far left connects with Stainby No. 5 quarry; main line in left centre leads to the BR High Dyke branch, which dealt exclusively with iron ore traffic. (G. Ordish)

INTRODUCTION AND ACKNOWLEDGEMENTS

'*Ironstone Railways and Tramways of the Midlands*', published in 1959 with a further edition of 1961 incorporating minor revisions, went out of print in a few years and—judging by the prices paid for secondhand copies—appears to have become something of a collector's item. This implication of a continuing interest in the subject is confirmed by the demand for photographs, greater than for most other kinds of industrial railway, doubtless largely because of the pleasant rural background of the ironstone lines.

I maintained my interest in ironstone by periodic visits to the working quarries, recording events as they happened, and pursuing research into the past as opportunity offered. On one of my visits to Sysonby Lodge, the area headquarters of Stewarts & Lloyds Minerals Ltd 'North of the Welland', the general manager, Tim Barclay, said; "Why don't you include information about quarry machines in a revised book? We have all the details of ours in the 'black book' and you are welcome to those." It proved to be one of the soundest pieces of advice I have had, and I spent a whole day transcribing exactly the data in the 'black book' that had yielded so much information on the locomotives in the past, and which was even better for quarry machines as it covered every one they had owned. A few months later this priceless record 'disappeared'—making me very thankful that I had been given the opportunity to obtain its information.

It set me thinking, too, and thus was born the idea of compiling a history on a wider basis than *IRTM*, an idea that gained momentum as the industry contracted; for here was an opportunity that could never come again. On the one hand, my long association with the industry in happier days, and friendship with so many of the people in it, whose knowledge complemented official sources; and, on the other, the vast increase in recent years of information available in county and British Steel Corporation archives. I have also been permitted to inspect much material (such as leases) in the private files of estate offices, solicitors and county planning authorities. Many friends who share my enthusiasm have also gone out of their way to help.

Transport has always played a vital part and is here given the same full treatment as in *IRTM*, for which no apology is made; but much more information is given on the history of the quarries—how they began and how they progressed—and the precise extent of quarrying, with dates where known. Details of quarry machines used in extracting the ironstone are tabulated in a manner similar to that used for locomotives. Finally, for the benefit of the industrial archaeologists who now, alas, will be the only visitors, there is a description of the sites as they are today. The research has revealed errors, misinterpretations and omissions in *IRTM*, and the text has been completely rewritten throughout, starting from original sources. Where doubt exists, I have said so.

Geographically, the area covered is shown in the the chronology section and is the same as in *IRTM*; the Scunthorpe district, with its complete interdependence between quarries and ironworks, is best studied as a unit, and the scattered ironstone quarries of the southwest (Wiltshire and Somerset) are again isolated and independent of East Midlands history.

The principal sources of information consulted, and quoted from throughout the book, using the abbreviations given, are:-

Mineral Statistics of Great Britain. Robert Hunt. Her Majesty's Stationery Office, 1853-1881   MS

Mineral Statistics of Great Britain. Geological Survey Memoirs. HMSO, 1882-1894   MS

List of Quarries in the United Kingdom and the Isle of Man. HMSO, 1895-1934   LQ

Special Reports on the Mineral Resources of Great Britain, Part XII-Iron Ores. Geological Survey Memoirs. HMSO, 1920   GSM

The Mesozoic Ironstones of England; the Northampton Sand Ironstone. Geological Survey Memoirs. HMSO. 1951   NSI

The Mesozoic Ironstones of England. The Liassic Ironstones. Geological Survey Memoirs. HMSO. 1952.   LI

Quarry work in earlier years was wholly manual, and this picture taken about 1910 at Desborough 'Co-Op' pits shows dramatically the back-breaking work, often only accepted in the lack of any other job.
(Desborough Cooperative Society)

The Quarries. H. B. Hewlett. The Stanton Ironworks
Co Ltd. 1935. Reprinted by the Rutland Railway
Museum. 1979.   Hewlett

Ryland's Iron, Steel, Coal and Tinplate Industries
Directory. 1881 onwards.   Rylands

Kelly's Directory for the counties concerned. Kellys

The basic source of information on quarry ownership in the 19th
century is Robert Hunt's *'Mineral Statistics'* published annually and
from 1882 under Government auspices. Hunt's records start (as far as
ironstone is concerned) in 1855 and are rather scanty for the first few
years; the impression is given that some of the early operators were
not anxious to publicise the site of their activities, and Mr Hunt did not
become aware of such beginnings immediately. There must have been
exploratory quarrying for all sorts of minerals going on all the time,
and he would only record those that had become established; up to
then, ironstone quarrying was unknown. So, before 1855, we have to
get our information from other sources, as detailed in the text. From
then onwards, Hunt's invaluable contemporary record has been widely
accepted; in the very few cases where I think another interpretation
is called for (e.g. Cranford; Fulbeck) I have been careful to indicate
clearly the reasons, so that readers can judge for themselves.

The format of MS was changed from 1895, but similar detailed
information continues in the *'List of Quarries'*. The lists are compiled
by H. M. Inspectors of Quarries, to whom all owners of quarries greater
than 20ft. in depth were obliged to report; shallow workings could be
recorded, but this was not obligatory, and a very few ironstone quarries
escaped mention in this way. The official publications listed as GSM,

Opposite page.
In the 20th Century machinery was increasingly introduced, first for removing
overburden, and then for digging the ironstone beneath. The picture taken in April
1960 at Market Overton's No. 6 Quarry, Rutland, shows a typical deep quarry with a
Ransomes & Rapier 5360 class electric stripping shovel removing the massive
Lincolnshire Limestone and a Ruston Bucyrus 110RB shovel (a rare type) loading
ironstone into wagons in the charge of Avonside locomotive ADDERLEY. Note in the
foreground the 'face ladder' and, on the top, a small dragline stripping topsoil and
putting it on a heap for replacement later.   (British Steel Corporation)

NSI and LI, compiled by teams of geologists with special local knowledge, are a treasure house of information; GSM describes all quarries of the World War I period, and the other two do the same for World War II, each with historical references also. Time and again, when queries have arisen, I have gone back to check the precise wording in these reports, and found them right. There is the accidental error of course — but we all make those, don't we?

Hewlett's book has a more general appeal, and is a gem; no doubt about it, a gem. He describes all the quarries owned by his company, Stanton Ironworks Co. Ltd, with a wealth of historical, topographical and geological detail in an easy, readable style. Hewlett was a surveyor; and no people are more knowledgeable on quarry history than the surveyors, as I soon came to appreciate. Indeed, it was Bill Jones — Hewlett's latter day counterpart at the former Stanton quarries 'North of the Welland' and a colleague of Tim Barclay's — who put me on the right way. I first got to know him well in the course of an 'in depth' study of Buckminster and Market Overton when these had been taken over by the railway preservation movement, to get the historical background of these schemes. The preservation efforts collapsed, but the research had been so fruitful that I decided to apply the same methods to ironstone quarries generally. It is true to say that this close association with the surveyors has been crucial in the preparation of this history, as they are involved in so many aspects of the business; dealing with landowners in the framing of leases, preparation of the site, making plans of every quarry at intervals of six months, advising on the types of machine required, and arranging for restoration on closure.

The most valuable documents from this source are the six-monthly surveys, and eventually all those that came within the ambit of Stewarts & Lloyds Minerals Ltd gravitated via Brigstock Manor and Syonsby Lodge (the Minerals offices south and north of the Welland) to Corby Regional Property Department. In addition to S&L proper and Stanton, former Staveley and South Durham quarries are included, and others. These will probably go to BSC Archives, but I was very privileged to be able to copy them in the surveyor's office, and thus to get answers to the queries inevitably raised. The major omission was the United Steels quarries based on the High Dyke line and here again the surveyor, Don Newman, then of Scunthorpe, duly provided the information. Future researchers studying these plans should take care to distinguish between 'take plans' and 'face plans'. The former indicate the area the operator proposed to take for working over the ensuing six to twelve months, and are denoted by straight lines, while the 'face plans' show the actual position of the working faces at the quoted date. The latter are clearly the more useful but if, as is sometimes the case, they are not available, the 'take plans' can be used, bearing in mind that the proposals to extract ore were occasionally unfulfilled. Examples of each type are reproduced overleaf.

These plans fill in the finer detail of quarry history, its annual progression, and incidentally indicate the changing layout of the tramways that served the working faces. Individual working faces or quarries were identified, sometimes by a number, more often by a name, and the origin of the names is a fascinating study in itself. Very often, especially in the small scale operations of early days, the old 'field names' were used, giving a link with local history. As working faces became bigger in the days of machinery, names indicative of a bigger area were used—the farm or the farmer, a village or a part of the estate. They do not often appear on surveyor's plans, but GSM, NSI and LI quote them freely, and so too do quarrymen; sometimes quarries were given more than one title, but which was official and which unofficial we do not always know. Company policy is often evident, too—quarries managed by Staveley started off by using field names, then used 'site' names of places or people; South Durham used site names almost exclusively, while Stanton, Holwell, and United Steels gave the quarries numbers mostly—much as they did with their locomotives. Hook Norton is particularly interesting, with the Partnership quarries named after local landowners, the Brymbo quarries given place names, and the Earl of Dudley's given field names.

Leases are of great value in indicating when and where quarrying was permitted, and the conditions appertaining, and fortunately a great number are preserved in county and BSC archives. They vary in detail but generally conform to a set legal pattern; and after a bit of experience the researcher can avoid the extreme tedium of reading every word (and my goodness, how difficult it is to follow lines in parallel three feet across!) by picking out salient words in larger characters, such as 'Habendum'. Later leases, printed on normal sized pages, are much easier to deal with. Particulars of rent and royalty payments are an essential part of the documents; in these books I have quoted royalties in a few instances, to give some idea of the 'going rate' at the time, but complete details are not given, as they are not often specially relevant and in some cases I have been asked not to quote

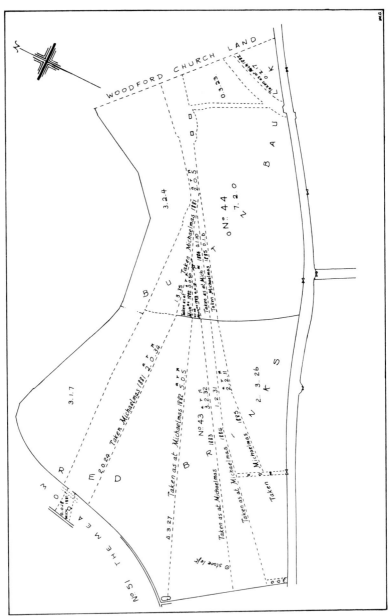

'Take' plan of Red Brinks Quarry, Woodford, Northamptonshire, showing the areas taken annually for ironstone extraction, 1881-85. This is before quarrying.

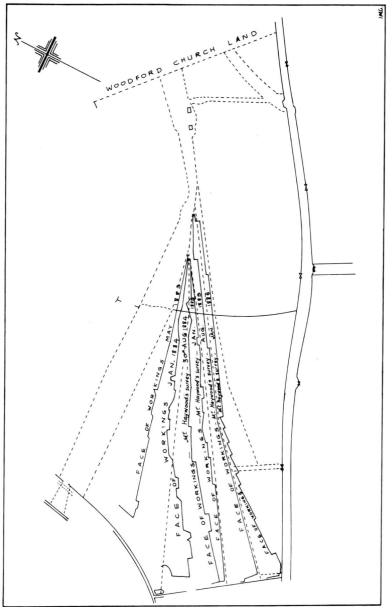

'Face' plan of Red Brinks Quarry, showing the position of the working faces at roughly half-yearly intervals, 1883-86. This is after quarrying.

the figures.

It has proved impossible to incorporate the much greater amount of information now available in one volume; instead the work will appear in several volumes, commencing with the Introduction and followed by a series devoted to specific areas, by county as far as practicable. Uniformity of presentation has however been the aim and the following comments are applicable to all volumes.

Throughout the text, 'quarry' means an opencast working, 'mine' an underground operation, irrespective of any local application of the latter term to opencast locations (e.g. United Steels at Cottesmore had COTTESMORE MINES painted on the locomotive tank sides). Shallow quarries were often referred to as 'pits' and in later years this term came to be associated more particularly with individual working faces within a quarry system, and as such has been used in the text, since it accords with local parlance. For example, at Irchester were Wembley Pit, Lodge Pit and Woolaston Pit, none of which could by any stretch of the imagination be called shallow; but I cannot recall ever having heard 'Lodge Quarry' used by the men there.

In the heading of sections I have, however, only used 'Quarries' or 'Mines' as appropriate and in general have adopted those names used in MS and other official sources. Where there was more than one operator in the same area, this has led to duplication, the main ones being Blisworth, Brixworth, Ditchford, Irthlingborough, Desborough, Holwell, Waltham, Caythorpe, Adderbury, Bloxham and Hook Norton; but reference to ownership will dispel any ambiguity. Where a location has been reopened by an entirely different company, I have usually dealt with them in the same section, an important exception being Manor Farm/Dean & Chapter/Irthlingborough, because of their historical significance.

In describing rail systems, I have used the word 'tramway', for which there is no generally accepted definition; in *IRTM* it was applied to lines used by an ironstone (or other) company, and 'railway' to lines owned by BR or its predecessors. In the present book I have adopted a similar distinction except in the case of a few latterday rail systems (e.g. Corby, Exton Park, Harlaxton, Oxfordshire Ironstone) where 'tramway' seems inappropriate; but the text, I hope, leaves no ambiguity.

On the maps the more permanent features of the tramway layouts are given and I have tried to show the areas of quarrying, with quarry names, dates and direction of movement of the working faces where known. From these the position of tramways serving them at any one time can be judged. Passing places, where known, are indicated, but there must be many of which no record has survived; nor can it be assumed that there was one on every branch, as it was common practice for a locomotive to propel empty wagons to the face and haul back the full ones without running round the train. The maps are based on the Ordnance Survey with the sanction of the Controller of HMSO, with additions from other sources for periods between successive editions of the OS. They have been drawn by Ian Lloyd, who hails from Corby and has a personal interest in the subject. I am greatly indebted to him, not only for preparing the maps, but also for pointing out errors in my original drawings.

At the end of each quarry's history is given the locomotive stock list, using the format adopted in the Industrial Railway Society Handbooks, plus leading dimensions. The basic information derives from the records of the Industrial Locomotive Society and Industrial Railway Society, modified by research at local level.

The majority of photographs are not of my taking, and are credited appropriately to the best of my knowledge: my grateful thanks are due to all who have kindly allowed me to use their work, with particular thanks to the British Steel Corporation for permission to use photographs from various sources within the organisation. Photographs credited B.G.S. are reproduced with the sanction of the Director, British Geological Survey/NERC; Copyright reserved.

Locomotives have been the subject of enthusiast attention for some 50 years, and the records of them are pretty comprehensive, apart from some very early locomotives about which we are now unlikely to learn more. Quarry machines, on the other hand, have had comparatively little attention, and gaps in our knowledge are inevitable. I have mentioned already how I came to acquire information on the machines of Stewarts & Lloyds Minerals Ltd 'North of the Welland', which was a very good start indeed; there were no comparable records for south of the Welland, nor for other operators, but the information has been forthcoming from senior personnel. Harold King had a card index of early Staveley machines, but had most of the information in his head anyway! Rutland Railway Museum have kindly supplied details, from official sources, of machines used in the United Steels quarries. The rest was obtained by going back to old quarrymen, and it soon became apparent that to most of them quarry machines were more familiar than locomotives; this in itself brought some regrets that I had not asked similar questions thirty years ago of old employees who have now passed on, taking their information with them. Finally, the principal manufacturers, Ruston Bucyrus Ltd and Ransomes and Rapier Ltd, have kindly allowed me to consult their files for details of all machines supplied to ironstone companies.

Most ironstone quarries used little in the way of fixed plant; buildings comprised only a few sheds and huts, while the quarries themselves and their associated tramways were subject to restoration requirements. In spite of these limiting factors there are few quarries that have not left **some** traces, and these are described, but changes are continually taking place in land usage, even in those few that had been left to the forces of nature. The descriptions apply to the early 1980's but in the case of the more important remains a date of last sighting is quoted. The aspect attracting the greatest enthusiast attention is the rail system, which often provides the most enduring remains anyway, in bridges, cuttings and embankments.

In addition to the principal sources listed, a number of periodicals and newspapers have been consulted, and extracts from these are acknowledged in the text, along with references to specialised sources such as archives, company and estate records, official files, society publications and technical books and booklets. Newspapers on the whole are not a rich source of information on quarries; sometimes, in early years, they mention the opening of a new quarry or the local council's permission for a tramway crossing of a road, and in the 1960's report the steady stream of closures. Otherwise they record mainly accidents and curiosities, but even these items are frequently useful in giving dates to particular workings. Searching newspaper files is very tedious, however, and while I have done plenty of it, I have been glad to take advantage of others who have combed the files and kindly let me use their findings—in particular Roger West, Mick Dix, and Geoffrey Starmer's team of industrial archaeologists. There are a few sources that I have not examined fully—the files of Companies House, those of the Public Record Office, and some newspapers not available locally. All these are very demanding of time, which for me is now not unlimited; but I mention them for the guidance of anyone interested in looking further into the history of any particular quarry.

The post-war years have witnessed a growing awareness of the importance of industrial archives, with company records saved instead of being thrown out for burning. This is particularly true of the British Steel Corporation, to whose East Midlands Regional Records Centre at

Irthlingborough I have paid numerous visits. There is also, as already mentioned, a vast amount of valuable archival material in the care of the BSC surveyors at Corby, to whom I owe special thanks—Norman Bellamy, Roy Dean, Jim Lees, George Naylor, Alan Pack; interested themselves, they went out of their way to help. "I'm sure we have something on this in the files; hang on while I have a look" they would say, as well as providing leads to information not indexed anywhere other than their own minds. The same goes for the archivists of the county record offices, patiently helping to track down information even if not on their own shelves. It is here where indebtedness to individuals comes in; so much the enquirer can find for himself by reading books and looking through files, or just using his eyes—but there is more that is not in the books or files, and not obvious to the eye. For the distant past we have to make do with what has been kept, but within living memory we can find out such a lot more to clothe the bare bones of statistics.

So much of this kind of research depends on the help of interested individuals; within the industry there are those who have saved company records which might otherwise have been destroyed, and kept them in the office or even in their homes; and there are quarrymen with long memories. The late Jack Roberts was one; sometimes his information could be checked against surveyors' records, and in such cases he was invariably right, so I had no hesitation in accepting his word on other matters where official confirmation was not available. Then there are the local historians whose interest embraces anything connected with a particular locality; it would be impossible to write about any aspect of Blisworth without mentioning George Freeston, or of Adderbury without 'J. J. Fox' appearing in the credits. With similar aims are the history societies, whose local knowledge is a great help to the specialist interested in any aspect of their area. There are hundreds of people whose help varies from expert knowledge of an area to the ability to answer the odd query; I have tried to give the credit due to them at the appropriate places in the text, as this seems more meaningful than one comprehensive list—and a long list it would be, to include everyone who has written or spoken to me. If through forgetfulness or ignorance I have omitted any acknowledgement, I can but apologise now.

To my great regret, I took few photographs, thereby losing many opportunities of recording events ordinary and extraordinary; I am deeply grateful to the photographers who have kindly permitted me to

19

make use of their work in this field.

In *IRTM* I spoke of the threefold joys of its compilation—"the satisfaction of discovery, the pleasure of tramping the countryside in all seasons, and the innumerable and invariably friendly contacts that alone have made the collection of information possible". My sentiments are the same today, plus a fourth dimension—thankfulness to God for the continuing excellent health that has enabled me to complete my researches, indoor and outdoor. It is equally gratifying to return home with a stack of information after a day poring over dusty files, or spent looking up old friends from the quarries, or just walking and observing. I have walked some 8,500 miles on ironstone exploration, and apart from occasional jaunts with kind friends by car (including a 1930 Morris Oxford!) all my visits have been by public transport. With Birmingham so excellently served by rail, there has never been any difficulty in covering the average 50 mile initial journey, and while dwindling country bus services have made some areas more difficult than formerly, most places are accessible by day trips, given good legs and lungs. The great majority of these outings have been solitary ones, with a flask of tea and a packet of marmalade sandwiches for sustenance, preferably somewhere with a sight to stir the memory. Any walk in the ironstone country recalls memories of previous visits, often of working quarries, and it is a happy fact that on these trips I am more likely to meet someone I know than in the centre of Birmingham.

To those who remember the working quarries it is even now hard to realise that they have all gone and that many people have never seen one. In these pages I have tried to recount their history as fully as possible, combining the facts and statistics from the records with an appreciation of the quarries as a working environment, a way of life that has now gone—at least in the case of the little railways—for ever. The archives will always be available for study, but the people who compiled them were mortal and took with them so much that is not recorded; and it is this combination of circumstances that has given me an opportunity that will not recur. I am very well aware that through inexperience I have not always made the best use of facilities so freely given and any shortcomings in the story must be ascribed to me.

Research never ends and I shall continue to study and visit the old quarry sites as long as I am able, if for no other reason than that the combination of physical and mental exercise brings great peace of mind. If readers who knew the quarries have fresh information to extend or amend what I have written, I shall be delighted to hear from them; and I shall be equally happy to help the younger enthusiasts who would like to know more. Of one thing I am certain—my interest in ironstone will remain with me for the rest of my days.

Finally, words can hardly express my indebtedness to Vera, who has never complained of the countless hours I have spent visiting the quarries and then writing about them; she must often have worried about my safety, particularly in recent years when I was scrambling round deserted sites in winter.

OUTLINE HISTORY OF
THE IRONSTONE INDUSTRY

Types of Iron Ore

Iron ore has been smelted in the British Isles for over 2000 years, and in the Industrial Revolution it became the most important mineral after coal, making the combination of the two vital to the economic security of the nation. The ore occurs in three principal forms; Hematite, a dull red heavy material, chemically ferric oxide, that formerly existed in large quantities in Cumberland and Furness and, though largely exhausted in Victorian times, was still mined in a few localities in this century and indeed outlived the bedded ores by a few months: Clay Ironstone, which in association with the Coal Measures, was the source of early Victorian industrial prosperity, again is mostly worked out: and the bedded ironstones collectively referred to by geologists as the Mesozoic iron ores, which form the subject of this book. These last differ widely in form, colour, purity and chemical composition and the geological history has been the subject of intensive research over many years.

In the geological period known as the Jurassic—chiefly known for its wealth of reptilian fauna—most of England was covered by shallow seas in which sediments were deposited over long periods of time, forming beds of rock many hundreds of feet thick; changes in the condition of these seas brought about by alterations in currents, coastline and vegetable and animal life forms, are reflected in the differing characteristics of the deposits, which form a number of well-defined beds or strata; and it is in the Liassic and Oolitic beds, together representing the latter half of the Jurassic Age, that the ironstone occurs; a small amount of ironstone was also deposited in the succeeding Cretaceous Age, but this was only of minor importance.

During the Cretaceous period most of Britain was still under the sea, and more detritus was slowly superimposed on the Jurassic rocks; but in geologically more recent times (Tertiary) the seas receded and the rock formations acquired a gentle slope from northwest to southeast, so that as the topmost portions were subsequently eroded away, the various beds were exposed in the order in which they were laid down, i.e. as one proceeds south-eastward each stratum disappears beneath succeeding layers. The Liassic and Oolitic strata that concern us form a broad outcrop stretching from North Yorkshire to Dorset, but to the east they disappear beneath later formations.

The Liassic beds are subdivided into a number of distinct formations varying in type and composition; the Lower Lias, characterised by a layered appearance from which—due to Somerset mis-pronunciation—arises its name, consists chiefly of grey limestone, blue shales and clays. In north Lincolnshire a rich bed of ore known as the Frodingham Ironstone occurs in this formation but further south it thins out and disappears; and the Liassic ironstone also occurs in the Marlstone beds of the overlying Middle Lias. The Marlstone Rock, in contrast to the blue-grey clays above and below, is warm red in colour and appears at the surface at many points stretching from Caythorpe in Lincolnshire to Wartnaby in Leicestershire; in the southern part it forms an imposing escarpment on which Belvoir Castle is a prominent feature. Further north, the Marlstone Rock iron ore is exposed between Grantham and Lincoln and to the south there is an isolated outcrop at Tilton, and the very extensive Oxfordshire field.

The Upper Lias comprises blue and grey shales and clays above which are the Oolitic beds, so-called from the fish-roe like grains that form a great part of the limestones in this formation. The series of the Lower Oolites consist of three main sub-divisions—the 'Northampton Sand' bed, the Lower Estuarine beds and the Lincolnshire Limestone (in ascending order), the different characteristics of which imply changes in the conditions obtaining when the rocks were deposited. Shallow seas, depositing relatively coarse material, gave rise to the Northampton Sand, which is the principal ironstone-bearing bed; the Estuarine series was formed (as the name implies) under brackish or freshwater conditions; and the limestone was laid down in quiet seas. The first two beds are very variable in thickness and compositon and consequently there is not a continuous bed of workable ironstone over the whole area where the Northampton Sand bed is accessible. As in the Marlstone Rock, the Lower Oolitic outcrop forms a striking landscape feature in the form of an escarpment (on which stand Lincoln Cathedral and Rockingham Castle) stretching from the Humber to Wilbarston in Northamptonshire; in general the Oolitic Cliff, as it is known, is not so steep or so high as the Marlstone escarpment but is much longer, and ironstone has been worked at many points along it. Further east and south these beds dip under later formations and no more ironstone is found apart from an isolated outcrop of ferruginous stone in the neighbourhood of Claxby, Lincolnshire, deposited in Cretaceous times.

The chemistry of the Mesozoic ironstones is extremely complex and the ore may be present in any of a wide variety of chemical combinations. The principal constituent is siderite, an impure ferrous carbonate, usually yellow or brown in colour; this is commonly associated with (and is probably derived by carbonation from) a mixed silicate of iron and aluminium known as chamosite, which is green in colour in the unoxidized state. Under oxidizing conditions, particularly where the stone outcrops, these two minerals are converted into limonite, a hydrated ferric oxide of the characteristic yellow-brown colour familiar to all who have watched a trainload of ore rumbling through a wayside station; limonite is the principal constituent of ironstone as quarried but is less evident in the output from deep quarries or mines. In spite of overall wide differences in composition, ironstones from each of the four geological formations show certain individual characteristics, enabling them to be classified into four types:-

1. **Frodingham ironstone**, occurring in the Lower Lias and quarried in the Frodingham area, is characterised by a high lime content (rendering the ore self-fluxing in the furnace) and low silica. It is usually mixed with a proportion of more siliceous Northampton Sand ore to form the furnace charge.

2. **Marlstone ironstone** from the Middle Lias is quarried in the Marlstone Rock from Caythorpe to Wartnaby, Tilton and the Oxfordshire Field with its outliers near Byfield and Charwelton in Northamptonshire. This contains more iron and generally less lime than the Frodingham ore, but the amounts of lime and silica vary in different localities, hence suitable ores are mixed in the furnace charge.

3. **Northampton Sand ironstone** from the Lower Oolites is quarried along the Oolitic Cliff from Greetwell (near Lincoln) to Rockingham and to the southeast—embracing much of Northamptonshire and Rutland—and also including the southeastern part of Northamptonshire from Kettering to Blisworth and eastward to a point where the stone becomes too poor to be workable. It is the richest of

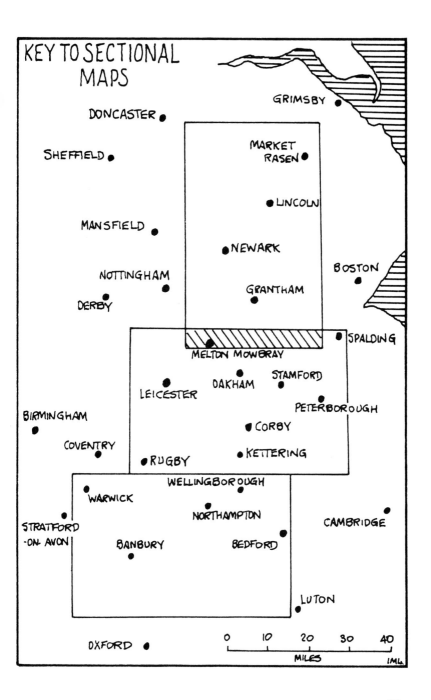

KEY TO SECTIONAL MAPS

GRIMSBY

DONCASTER

SHEFFIELD

MARKET RASEN

LINCOLN

MANSFIELD

NEWARK

NOTTINGHAM

BOSTON

DERBY

GRANTHAM

SPALDING

MELTON MOWBRAY

STAMFORD

OAKHAM

LEICESTER

PETERBOROUGH

BIRMINGHAM

CORBY

COVENTRY

KETTERING

RUGBY

WELLINGBOROUGH

WARWICK

NORTHAMPTON

CAMBRIDGE

STRATFORD -ON AVON

BANBURY

BEDFORD

LUTON

OXFORD

0   10   20   30   40

MILES

IML

the ores in iron content but is siliceous and needs the addition of lime or a lime-rich ore as a flux before being charged into the furnace.

4. **Claxby ironstone** from the Lower Cretaceous, mined only at Nettleton near Claxby, Lincolnshire. Similar to Marlstone ore but poorer in iron and rather siliceous.

KEY

———o——— CORBY	Main line railway with station
++++++++++++++	Main line mineral railway
....	County boundary
⊥⊥⊥⊥⊥⊥⊥⊥⊥⊥	Canal
⊤ ⊤ ⊤ ⊤ ⊤	Northampton Sand
• • • • • • • • •	Marlstone Rock
– • — • — • — •	Claxby Ironstone
⋅⋅⎮⎮⎮⎮⎮⎮⎮⎮⎮⎮⎮⎮⎮⎮⎮⎮⎮⎮⎮⎮⎮	Escarpment

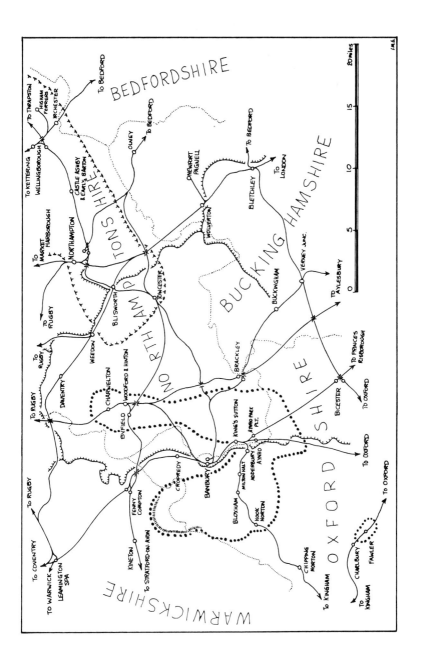

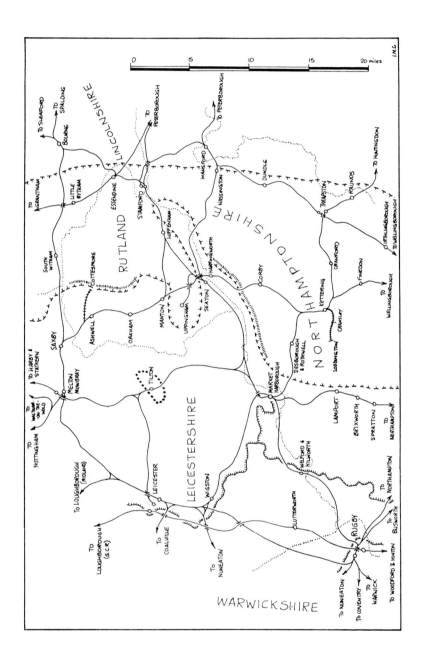

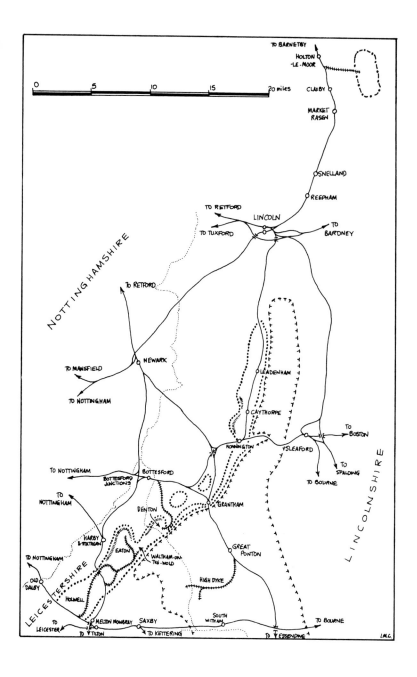

Origins of the East Midlands Iron Ore Industry

It is not known when iron was first produced from its ores, but the process was carried out in various parts of Europe for many centuries B.C., and in the British Isles there is evidence that iron was produced about 200 B.C., probably in a primitive type of low hearth similar to the Catalan furnace still found in the Pyrenees; Caesar, in *'De Bello Gallico'*, reports the use of iron rings for money and iron rims to chariot wheels. The metal was smelted mostly in the maritime regions, though finds of iron objects were made elsewhere, including Hunsbury Hill in Northamptonshire.[1] The period of Roman Occupation, however, saw considerable expansion in iron production and improvements in the process of smelting, and in many places there are traces of the industry dating back to this time. Smelting sites have been found at Irchester and Kettering in Northamptonshire and at several of the locations that later supplied ore to Corby Works (Corby, Gretton, Rockingham, Wakerley); at Market Overton in Rutland; and at Frodingham and Colsterworth in Lincolnshire. New sites are continually being discovered as a result of archaeological exploration. After the departure of the Legions, the industry continued to flourish and in the time of Edward Confessor there are records of 'Ferrarrii' (iron forges or ironworks) at Corbei and Gretone, and they are mentioned in the *Domesday Book*.[2] Rockingham Castle, which occupies a commanding position on the Oolitic Escarpment where so much mineral wealth lies buried, dates from Norman times and is believed to have been built for the protection of the royal forges. Throughout Medieval times the demand for iron increased, the principal ironmaking centres being the Weald of Kent, Sussex and Rockingham Forest; amongst others, there are records of furnaces at Geddington from the time of Henry II to Henry III.[3]

The ores were reduced to the metal by smelting with wood charcoal, a ready supply of which was obtainable from the forest underwood; this phase of the industry reached its peak in the 17th century. It is here necessary to refute an oft-repeated myth (which we confess having in ignorance helped to perpetuate in *IRTM*) that the cessation of ironmaking in the Midlands was due to laws forbidding the making of charcoal in certain areas because of the destruction of forest trees; but charcoal burning used readily renewable underwood, not mature trees and the ironworks lasted as long as those of the 19th and 20th centuries were to do. The destruction of the woods was then (as it still is) due far more to the spread of agriculture. The decline of the inland iron forges was due to a much simpler reason, and one that was to be repeated more than once in the period we shall be studying; the import of better grade ores more cheaply from overseas, notably Sweden. (see *Trees and Woodland in the British Isles'* by Oliver Rackham. Dent, 1976).

In the mid-18th century the home ironmaking industry was given impetus by the introduction of coke as fuel, and numerous ironworks sprang up in the coal-producing districts, where iron ore was found in close association. The existence of iron ore in the East Midlands was for practical purposes forgotten, or at any rate neglected, and the story of its rediscovery in the early 19th century would make a fascinating study in itself; we have come across several references in the course of research and there must be others that would give a clearer picture. Our first is dated about 1815, when a Mr Corefield of Northampton forwarded samples to Mr Mushet, apparently without raising that eminent ironfounder's enthusiasm; Corefield subsequently moved to Cheltenham and presumably lost interest in and credit for a discovery of cardinal importance. (see *Mining Journal,* 11th February 1855, p.762). Another is that of S. H. Blackwell, who noted ironstone, again in the vicinity of Northampton, about 1843. Surveys for the building of the Midland Railway 'Leicester & Hitchin Branch' revealed near Desborough the existence of ironstone that the company recognised as of economic importance. Without any doubt, the railways were primarily responsible for the commercial development of the Mesozoic iron ores, both by creating a greatly increased demand and by providing the means of transporting the ore to the ironworks when the available iron ores of the Coal Measures were largely exhausted, and the ironmasters were looking for other sources.

The East Midlands ironstone industry can be said to have had its beginnings at the Great Exhibition of 1851, when samples of ironstone from various parts of Britain were shown, including specimens from the estate of Colonel Arbuthnot at Woodford, near Thrapston, Northamptonshire; this gentleman had sent samples for examination by Dr. Perry of Birmingham, and he in turn passed them to Mr. Blackwell, who visited the county and collected specimens for the Exhibition.[4] Events followed rapidly; Mr. Thomas Butlin erected an experimental furnace at Northampton and smelted local ore for the

31

first time in February 1852 — a sample running used to be preserved in Northampton Museum — and later that year started to set up his ironworks at East End, on the outskirts of Wellingborough.[5]

Footnotes:

[1] R. D. Smith in J. W. Mellor's '*A comprehensive treatise on Inorganic and Theoretical Chemistry*' 1947. Vol. 12, p.500.

[2] Dr John Evans: Address to the Antiquarian Section of the Iron and Steel Institute, Northampton, 1878.

[3] J. W. Judd: *Geology of Rutland etc. Geological Survey Memoirs, 1874.* p.110.

[4] S. H. Blackwell: *Ironmaking resources of the United Kingdom.* British Iron Trade Association Journal, 7th April 1852, p.384.

[5] W. H. Butlin, M.A.: *The Northampton Iron Ore District.* Journal of the Iron & Steel Institute, May 1883, p.186. See also Mining Journal, 11th January 1868, p.31.

Development of the Industry in the 19th Century

Most spheres of human activity are not properly recognised or recorded until they have become established, and the beginnings are often difficult to discover; so it is with the iron ore industry, recorded assiduously by Robert Hunt in *'Mineral Statistics'* from the middle 1850's. Blisworth is the first site to be mentioned and as a result this priority has been stressed, while earlier contenders that escaped mention in MS have been overlooked; these were at Hardingstone, near Northampton and Manor Farm, near Wellingborough.

In the earlier quarries the ore was outcropping or very close to the surface with only a thin covering of soil, and for commercial exploitation had to be close to means of transport to ironworks at a considerable distance. In practice this meant railways, the key role of which is well shown by the disposition of the first quarries; at that time the only railways in Northamptonshire were the London & North Western Railway main line from London to the northwest, and the long Blisworth-Peterborough branch; some of the earliest quarries in the county lay along the latter like a string of beads—Hardingstone, Duston, Cogenhoe, Manor Farm. Two more (Gayton and Lodge Plantation) were served by the main line. While railways were then recognised as the most convenient means of moving heavy material in bulk, the Canal Age had not been forgotten, and the first quarries at Blisworth used canal transport, though admittedly this was because direct access to the LNWR was difficult.

The first quarries in Leicestershire and Oxfordshire were short-lived 'one-offs' just because they happened to be near existing transport facilities; in Oxfordshire there was the extraordinary outpost of Fawler alongside the Oxford, Worcester & Wolverhampton Railway, and the first Adderbury pit by the Oxford Canal, while the first Leicestershire quarry was the isolated Nevill Holt served by the LNWR Rugby-Peterborough line. Otherwise, events followed the same pattern as in Northamptonshire, with commercial development entirely dependent on additions to the railway network. The potential of the Marlstone Rock was recognised but lack of transport facilities held up exploitation in Leicestershire and Oxfordshire until 1875 and 1889 respectively. The first Lincolnshire workings, excluding the Frodingham Field, were in the northern part, at Claxby (1868), Greetwell (1873) and Caythorpe

After being dug from the quarry, the ironstone had to be transported to the ironworks, usually involving a journey by main-line railway. The transfer arrangements differed to suit local conditions; here, loaded tubs on the 1ft. 9½in. gauge tramway from Stanton Ironworks Co Ltd quarry at Holwell, Leicestershire, are lowered singly to a tipping device over the siding on the LMSR Holwell Branch, which was constructed by the Midland Railway solely to serve the local ironstone quarries. This view was taken in 1934.(Stanton Ironworks Co Ltd)

Where quarries were served by a standard gauge line, loaded wagons could be taken directly to the main line sidings by the quarry locomotive, as shown, with locomotive 11 (Andrew Barclay 1047) pushing wagons into the BR sidings at Storefield quarries on the Kettering-Corby line, 15th August 1968.

(G. H. Starmer)

(1880 onwards), with later quarrying south towards the Rutland border; in Rutland itself Cottesmore was opened in 1882, all the rest dating from the 20th century. In Northamptonshire the trend was mainly from south to north and from west to east. The isolated Warwickshire quarry at Burton Dassett dates from 1868.

The Staffordshire ironmasters of the mid-19th century were not slow to investigate the possibilities of supplementing their dwindling reserves of Blackband (Clay) ironstone from a relatively close source of ore but in the main they failed to persevere in adapting their methods to Northamptonshire ore, which requires a different furnace technique, and their results at first were disappointing. Eventually these technical difficulties were overcome but not much Northamptonshire ore went to Staffordshire at any time; this may have been partly due to early prejudices but more likely to the convenient access from the Oxfordshire field as the latter was opened up. Northamptonshire supplied mainly Derbyshire, Nottinghamshire, South Yorkshire and South Wales—and furnaces erected in the ironstone field itself. The Marlstone ore of Leicestershire went almost exclusively to the ironworks of Derbyshire and Nottinghamshire (notably Stanton and Staveley) and to Holwell Works, at Asfordby, Leicestershire. Further east, an increasing amount of Northampton Sand ironstone, particularly from Rutland and Lincolnshire, went to the Scunthorpe area for admixture with the local Frodingham ore. Most British native iron ores contain phosphorus, making them unsuitable for steel manufacture, for which process non-phosphoric ores had to be imported from Sweden or Spain; but Gilchrist Thomas patented a process by which steel could be made from phosphorus-containing ores, which was introduced successfully in 1879 in this country and elsewhere.

Up to about 1900, with hand labour general throughout the industry, the emphasis was on finding and working ironstone as close to the surface as possible; and as these outcrop workings near the railways became exhausted, areas further away were opened up, with correspondingly longer hauls by tramway to the main lines. As additions to the rail networks were made, quarries sprang up alongside them to develop fresh areas of stone under shallow cover; for examples, the MR Kettering-Cambridge and Kettering-Manton lines: LNWR/GNR Joint Line Melton Mowbray-Nottingham: GWR Kings Sutton-Chipping Norton. The next development was the building of special mineral branches by the main line companies to areas where large reserves of ironstone, capable of generating worthwhile traffic, were known to exist. The first example was the rather remote branch of the Manchester, Sheffield and Lincolnshire Railway to serve the Acre House mine in the Claxby area (1868) but the major ironstone branches were all begun in the decade 1877-87; these comprised the MR branches to Cransley (1877—extended to Loddington 1891), Holwell (1879) and Cottesmore (1882), then the GNR lines to Waltham-on-the-Wolds (1882), Woolsthorpe (1884, extended to Denton 1885), Eaton (1885); this last was linked to the MR Holwell Branch by the extension of the latter to Wycomb Junction (1887). It will be noted that with the exception of Loddington in Northamptonshire, these lines lay in the eastern half of the ironstone district, where there were few main line railways.

Development of the Industry in the 20th Century

From 1900 the pattern of development changed; the availability of machinery to do the hard work of removing overburden (the depth of soil above the ironstone bed) meant that quarrying was no longer limited to the 25ft. commonly regarded as the maximum workable by hand labour (the 40ft. said to have been shifted at Newbridge Quarry was very much an exception); so that instead of going further afield to get ore under shallow cover—which was becoming ever more difficult anyway—it was possible to get it by digging deeper. Lloyds Ironstone Co Ltd at Corby was the first firm to introduce such

The early quarries were of necessity all shallow and in some areas working under thin cover was possible over long periods, thanks to uniform conditions. Our picture shows a line of hopper wagons being loaded at No. 8 Quarry, Buckminster, Lincolnshire, by a 43RB diesel dragline after the latter has removed the overburden. The scene is typical enough, but the locomotive is IRONSTONE, Peckett 1050, which Stanton's records do not show as being here, and her stay was evidently only a very short one, 1939-40. (F. Cooper)

machinery, but the best example of the new approach is Market Overton, opened in 1906 on the new MR Saxby-Bourne line, and operated by machinery right from the start. Almost all quarries opened after this used machinery throughout, and most of the 19th century sites still operating brought in machinery as the cover increased; a very few, such as Burton Latimer and Wartnaby, kept on with hand labour to the end in the 1920's. Mechanical removal of overburden was quickly followed by mechanical loading of ironstone and in later years was general. Throughout all these changes, connections to main line railways continued, the most frequently used being the pioneer LNWR Blisworth-Peterborough line, with some 20 quarries served in all.

The ability to win ore at much greater depths greatly extended the life of any quarry, and some old sites were reopened and extended

In contrast to the previous picture, we have the artifical 'Grand Canyon' of Lodge Pit, Irchester, Northamptonshire. To the right the 5360 Stripping Shovel is removing the deep overburden and dumping it on the worked-out ground to the left, where a small dragline is smoothing it over. On the quarry floor the locomotive stands at the ironstone face, and behind it the loading shovel is digging the ironstone. 23rd July 1962.   (S. A. Leloux)

Many early quarries, closed when the stone near the surface had been exhausted, were reopened for deeper working with the benefit of heavy machinery. Such an area was Blisworth, near Northampton, reopened in World War II after being closed for twenty years or more. In the foreground is BLISWORTH No. 1 (Andrew Barclay 2365 of 1955) standing on track well below road level, the ore having been extracted over the whole area in view. Note in the background the bridge under the Tiffield road, with loco shed alongside. To the left of this can just be seen the tunnel mouth used by the former narrow gauge tramway that served this area. Photograph taken March 1956.

(G. H. Starmer)

(Blisworth; Storefield; Wakerley; Eaton; Adderbury); but expansion into new areas was constantly being sought to keep pace with demand. Only two more mineral branches were built — the GNR High Dyke line, very successful and destined to carry enormous tonnages; and the Edge Hill Light Railway, a disastrous failure, partly because of its rope-worked incline. By this time, more lengthy lines to workings were commonplace, with the ironstone companies prepared to put these in themselves (Exton Park; Harlaxton; Wroxton).

The ironstone industry was always a very sensitive barometer of national economic conditions when the latter were strongly dependent on coal and iron; in difficult times these twin industries were depressed, ironstone quarrying along with them. All quarries suffered from this stop/start feature of the economy, with opening of quarries increasing in good times and closures prevailing in bad. The early 1890's was one difficult period, but the most serious was the post-World

War I depression, when dozens of quarries went out of production. Wartime was a time of expansion for obvious reasons and World Wars I and II show this trend very strongly. The post-World War II period was one of prosperity too, continued in the 1950's, with economic pressures directed towards labour-saving devices in increased mechanisation; but the 1960's ushered in a rapid contraction as iron and steel declined in importance. The ironworks within the ironstone field were closed in fairly quick succession (Kettering, Cransley, Wellingborough, Holwell) leaving only the integrated iron and steel plant at Corby. There were similar closures among the older ironworks in the Midlands, Yorkshire, Lancashire and South Wales that had relied mainly on East Midlands ironstone for a century, and by 1970 the remaining quarries in Northamptonshire and Lincolnshire were supplying Corby and Scunthorpe respectively.

The introduction at Scunthorpe and Redcar of the new 'LD' process of steelmaking, requiring the use of foreign ores richer in iron and with less lime and phosphorus, extinguished the demand for ironstone from the quarries 'North of the Welland'—Buckminster, Market Overton, Colsterworth, Woolsthorpe, Harlaxton; an ill-fated attempt to revive Harlaxton by supplying ore to two of the remaining Midlands ironworks (Bilston and Shelton) came to grief on technical difficulties, and the ironworks were soon closed anyway, leaving Corby Works as the sole market for Midlands ore. It seemed unthinkable even in the mid-1970's that Corby Works, on which the prosperity of the town depended, could be closed; but the sad history of other works of similar local significance, eg Consett, showed that it was all too likely; and so it came about on 4th January 1980 that the last load of Midlands iron ore trundled down the line from Harringworth to Corby.

QUARRY MANAGEMENT AND EQUIPMENT

Acquisition of land

The Mesozoic ironstones occur as beds, in working quarries averaging 10-12ft. in thickness, though up to 25ft. or more has been recorded in exceptional cases; it is generally uneconomic to work thinner layers, in which the stone is also usually poorer. These layers appear at the surface as outcrops in a few places, which were the first to be

Up to about 1900 all quarries relied entirely on manual labour, using the familiar 'plank and barrow' method of removing the overburden to expose the ironstone and dumping the former on the worked-out ground. This scene, taken at Wartnaby, Leicestershire, 20th September 1908, is typical. As the stone went deeper below the surface, it became necessary to remove the overburden in two stages, as shown. Note the flimsy trestles supporting the planks; the narrow gauge tubs at the face; the cuts in the stone by individual diggers; and the steam from the locomotive, just out of sight!

(B.G.S.)

Our view at Harlaxton No. 2 Quarry, Lincolnshire, taken in April 1963, shows the steps of working in strips by machines. To expose the top of the ironstone the 100RB dragline in the foreground is removing the rocky overburden in two stages, depositing the material on the worked-out ground to the left, where it will be smoothed over by the smaller machine and the topsoil eventually replaced. The rail track is laid at the base of the ironstone for the last 'cut' and the wagons loaded by a 54RB shovel in the distance. Deep quarries such as this were frequently under water in wet seasons.

(B.S.C)

recognised and exploited, otherwise they lie under an overburden that in later quarries reached 100ft. or more in depth, for which mechanical excavation was essential. Because of the relative thinness of the layers, the stone is removed in a series of parallel strips, the overburden from each being deposited on the previous one from which the iron ore had been removed. The working area was therefore continually changing, giving the ironstone quarries their most characteristic feature and focussing attention on them in later years, when land usage was regarded as more important than formerly.

Because the land for ironstone extraction was required only for a limited period, quarrying was exercised in the vast majority of cases by leasing a designated area for a specific period from the landowner, who was paid a rent for the land, a royalty for any mineral extracted and a wayleave in respect of the carriage of ores from any other sources. For ironstone the royalty was usually in the region of 3 to 6 old pence per nominal ton (commonly 2400 lbs) but varied over much wider limits; the wayleave was usually less than one penny per ton. In some cases, operators purchased the freehold of the land. As the industry got into its stride there was considerable competition among the major operators for good quality ore, and landowners were able to select from the more lucrative terms offered. As British agriculture was seriously depressed in the last quarter of the 19th century, such land was cheap, and this type of transaction a boon to some impoverished estates; but as land values rose and inflation also, long term leases were less favourable to landowners. Both operators and landowners formed protective associations to look after their common interests—the National Council of Associated Iron Ore Producers and the Ironstone Royalty Owners' Association.

Prospecting for ironstone usually took the form of making 'trial holes' on likely ground by arrangement with the landowner and/or occupier, and analysing the samples from various depths. If these proved satisfactory over a worthwhile area, a lease would be sought. If the area concerned lay some distance from the nearest railway, it was often necessary to secure a wayleave from another landowner enabling a tramway to be laid over his land.

The progress of quarrying was monitored by the surveyors who, usually at six-monthly intervals, drew plans of the working faces; fortunately for historians, a great many of these most valuable records survive in archives.

Quarry Ownership

The earliest quarries were owned by individuals or small companies but these were nearly all taken over before long by one of the ironmaking companies, who increasingly took the initiative in the opening of new quarries. A few landowners had a go at operating quarries on their own land but by and large these were either shortlived or taken over by one of the ironworks. The majority of workings came to be owned or controlled by ironworks in Derbyshire, Nottinghamshire, Yorkshire and Staffordshire and of course the Scunthorpe area of Lincolnshire and in the East Midlands ironstone field itself (Stowe; Heyford; Irthlingborough; Wellingborough; Finedon; Islip; Kettering; Cransley; Corby; Holwell). Each had its own policy regarding development and this was reflected at quarry level; these characteristics will be described in the text but we can mention a well-known example. Stanton Ironworks and Staveley Ironworks were two of the most influential owners from Victorian times; Stanton quarries were controlled from headquarters and locomotives and machines came to the ironworks shops for major overhauls, often going to different quarries afterwards, as a result of which there was continual interchange of stock, but a fair degree of standardisation achieved. Staveley's quarries were nearly all owned jointly with other companies (James Oakes; Bestwood; Park Gate etc) with Staveley exercising management; each quarry was nominally independent and expected to stand on its own feet by supplying ore to the works at an agreed price. There was greater individuality between the Staveley quarries, and fewer exchanges of equipment, but the Staveley hallmarks were still apparent. Mergers and takeovers tended to blur some of the distinctions and in the case of Eaton district it is quite impossible to relate the last few years' activity simply to previous owners; but such instances were few.

There were a few independent operators, the best known being James Pain, who owned half a dozen quarries in Northamptonshire and Rutland until taken over by Stanton in 1928; divisions within the family did not help, but independence would probably have ceased anyway during the Depression. The last 'independent', Nassington Barrowden Mining Co Ltd. was owned by Naylor Benzon & Co Ltd, who were large importers of foreign ore, and who took advantage of the upsurge in demand in World War II by opening three quarries in the East Midlands.

Under the Iron & Steel Act, 1949, all iron ore properties, the output of which went for iron production, were placed under national ownership in the form of the Iron & Steel Corporation of Great Britain; on the vesting date, 15th February 1951 the firms concerned became subsidiaries of the Corporation but continued to trade under their own names. The industry was denationalised under the Iron & Steel Act, 1953, the properties of the Corporation being transferred on 13th July 1953 to the Iron & Steel Holding and Realisation Agency, from which some companies repurchased their former properties; in the case of the Sheepbridge Co Ltd, their holdings were acquired by Staveley Iron & Chemical Co Ltd. Apart from a small amount of pooling of management and equipment, however, there were few outward changes. In 1968 the ten quarries and one mine remaining in production were taken over by the British Steel Corporation; these were owned or controlled by Stewarts & Lloyds Minerals Ltd (Irchester; Storefield; Corby; Market Overton; Buckminster; Woolsthorpe; Harlaxton) or by United Steel Companies Ore Mining Branch (Colsterworth; Exton Park; Sproxton; and Nettleton Mine). The USC properties were taken over 1st July 1968, the S&LM properties on 29th March 1970, when there was a general reorganisation of BSC. The independent quarries at Twywell (Pipewell Ploughing Co Ltd) and Nassington (Nassington Barrowden Mining Co Ltd) were outside the scope of the new Act but did not survive long.

Quarry Operation

Working by hand labour obtained in all ironstone quarries up to 1895, and lasted in many up to about 1920, the standard method being that familiarly known as 'plank and barrow'. The top soil and shallow overburden were removed from a long strip to expose the ironstone, which was then dug out and taken away; work then proceeded by similar strips, the overburden being loaded into barrows and trundled along planks supported on trestles, over the exposed ironstone face, to be dumped on the worked-out ground beyond. This hazardous occupation was general throughout the industry, with variants to suit local conditions; 'toppers' (a term used in the Oxfordshire quarries) became accustomed to the rythmic bounce of the planks, which soon became grooved from the iron-tyred barrow wheels, but they were preferred to new planks that lacked flexibility at first. The ironstone was loosened by picks and then usually loaded into wagons running on narrow gauge tracks; the tools for the men working at the face were pick, hammer, shovel and wide-tined fork. If the rock was very hard, which was often the case with the Marlstone Rock, blasting was necessary to loosen the stone for the loaders. Otherwise, a common practice was for the stone at the base to be loosened by pick over several yards of face, with a lookout man perched on the top to note the telltale cracks in the surface presaging collapse along the marked length; whereupon he would warn the men below to jump clear—while he did likewise! Plenty of scope for accidents in those days before the Health and Safety at Work Act! The ore was then loaded into narrow gauge tramway tubs and hauled to the main line railway or to the ironworks. As transport played so vital a part in the industry, and is the aspect of it that has attracted the most enthusiast attention, it is discussed in more detail in the next section.

The practice of calcining, ie roasting of ore admixed with coal slack to increase the iron content by driving off water and by chemical change, was performed in many quarries to reduce transport costs, particularly where the ore had to be transported long distances. At many sites it was introduced about the turn of the century, and reached its peak during World War II, after which it declined and came to an end in the early 1960's. The calcining was usually done in open-air 'clamps', sometimes on the quarry floor, sometimes on a level space

The men at Hurst's Quarry, Eaton, Leicestershire, were probably quite happy to have a moment's respite from their toil as the photographer took this view from a wheelbarrow plank, probably in the 1920's. Yet, from the operator's viewpoint, these were almost ideal conditions — a level site, a deep ironstone face with only a few feet of cover. Note the worked-out ground to the right, some twenty feet below the level of the roadside hedge, ready for cultivation. (B.S.C.)

From about the turn of the century the practice of calcining was introduced at many quarries. In this process the ore is mixed with coal slack in heaps and burnt for several weeks, at the end of which the iron content has risen by loss of moisture and by chemical change, thus reducing transport costs. The photograph shows this in progress at Buckminster No. 5 (Stainby) Quarry; the far end is burning well, and the near end cooling off, with wagons ready for loading. Note the avenue of trees in the background, typical of the Dysart Estate. Photograph taken 26th May 1945.

(B.G.S.)

The digger stands out starkly against a background of steam and smoke as it shovels up the burnt ore in the foreground for loading. The ore is by now a dark red and at the end of a day's work in these Stygian conditions the workers 'looked like Red Indians'. This evocative photograph was taken about 1930 in Gawthrupps Quarry, Glendon, Northamptonshire.   (Collection G. F. Barnes)

In the Banbury area, calcining was usually carried out in kilns resembling blast furnaces in some ways. Coke and ore were carried to the tops of the kilns and the load fired at the base. The view shows the single kiln at the Earl of Dudley's quarry at Hook Norton, Oxfordshire, with the tramway feeder in the foreground, in 1906.
                                        (Oxfordshire County Libraries)

Only a small proportion of Midlands ore emanated from mines, and those at Greetwell, near Lincoln, were the longest-lived, some sixty years. The galleries were served throughout by horse-operated narrow gauge tramways, the use of both steam and diesel locomotives proving unsatisfactory. Our picture of Long Harry Mine in September 1933, clearly shows the ironstone bed from tramway level to the top of the tunnel, with Lincolnshire Limestone above. Note the props used for roof support. (B.G.S.)

next to the loading sidings; an interesting variant, confined to quarries in the Banbury area, was the use of specially designed kilns of steel with refractory lining. Yet another variant, the brick-built kiln, was erected at Wakerley in Northamptonshire, but was never brought into use. Calcining reduced transport costs but was in itself labour-intensive, with double loading and extra locomotives required, which led to its abandonment in the post-war years.

Mining, as opposed to quarrying, though never a common practice in the ironstone fields, took place from very early days (Cogenhoe; Woodford; Acre House; Fawler) as an alternative to removing heavy cover; these were all small and shortlived concerns, but about 1878 mining on a larger scale commenced at Greetwell, near Lincoln. Other mines followed in the 20th century — Islip (1902), Cranford (1908),

As Greetwell Mines declined to exhaustion, the mines at Nettleton, north of Market Rasen, were opened up and rapidly expanded. Most of the motive power was provided by a fleet of diesel locomotives by Ruston & Hornsby, who indeed used the mines to test new designs. The 1959 photograph shows a class LBU in use. These mines are interesting in being in the small Claxby formation of the Cretaceous age, much younger than the Jurassic ores of the Northampton Sand and Marlstone Rock. On closure, the adits such as those shown were bricked up and today are visible reminders of past industry. The adit on the right was used for storing a Ruston locomotive and wagons, but the tunnel collapsed and they are still buried there. (Ruston & Hornsby)

Thingdon and Finedonhill (1909), Irthlingborough (1920) and Nettleton (1930). All these mines were adits driven into the hillside and accommodating narrow gauge tracks, and were worked by 'pillar and stall', with pillars of stone being left between galleries to support the roof. Mines, however, incur problems, technical and administrative, absent from opencast quarrying, in maintaining tunnels and other works in compliance with mines regulations and because of variability in the overlying strata; these restrictions led wherever possible to the practice of working opencast with massive overburdens in preference to mining, and some former mining areas (Wellingborough; Cranford) were in later years reopened in this way. There were two mines from the post-World War II period, Thistleton and Easton, but they only lasted a few years because of technical problems and excessive costs.

A memory of the past. A Barclay locomotive at No. 15 quarry, Buckminster, Lincolnshire, with its train of tipplers being loaded by a Ruston Bucyrus dragline. This site is close to Buckminster Hall, and across the valley lie Sproxton quarries, in Leicestershire. October 1963. (BSC)

Horse traction was commonly used on the earlier and smaller narrow gauge tramways. The photograph shows a typical setup at Gayton Wood Quarries, Northamptonshire, about 1908. Note how shallow is the pit, with perhaps only a couple of feet of cover. (Collection G. Freeston)

Even shallow quarries were mechanised in later years, but fairly small machines sufficed. The photograph shows a train in Kettering Quarries with a Manning Wardle locomotive, a 43RB diesel shovel loading the wooden wagons, and a small dragline removing overburden at the far end of the pit. September 1961. (G. P. Roberts)

At Wellingborough Quarries, ore under heavy cover had been won by mining from about 1910, but as larger machines became available it was possible to work opencast. This view was taken at No. 6 Quarry towards the end of operations, 2nd June 1966. A 55RB diesel shovel loads tubs in the charge of Peckett 1870. The tubs, two on a common frame, were lifted by crane at the ironworks. The limitation of the narrow gauge is apparent; a larger loader could fill a standard gauge wagon with the same number of lifts. (P. H. Groom)

Transport

All iron ore had to be carried to the ironworks, some direct from quarries to such works located in the ironstone fields, but much more to furnaces further away, involving main line railways. The preferred method in early days was the narrow gauge tramway with horses for haulage, though for some very short lines pushing by hand may have sufficed. Tramways to the standard gauge of 4ft. 8½in. as used on main line railways were sometimes put in, as at Duston (1854) right to the working face, in others only part way, usually to the foot of a narrow gauge rope-worked incline from the quarry (Hardingstone (1851);

Rope-worked inclines were a common feature of the narrow gauge tramways, to convey ore from hilltop quarries to railways in the valley. One of the most spectacular was at Eastwell, Leicestershire, where the wagons were clipped singly to the rope and lowered down the Marlstone escarpment to the LNWR/GNR Joint line at the bottom. This view was taken about 1953. (K. Cooper/IRS Collection)

Cogenhoe (1858); Nevill Holt (1861) etc). Inclines were common, as ironstone was frequently exposed as outcrop on escarpments; these were usually worked by the funicular principle whereby descending loaded wagons brought up empties at the other end of the cable, which passed over rollers between the rails and round a drum at the top, with

Canal transport of iron ore was mostly confined to the Blisworth area of Northamptonshire. Wagons from Phipp's quarries near the Courteenhall road were stopped on the bridge and the end lifted by crane to enable the load to be discharged through a gap in the planking to the barge below. The post of the crane is visible. On closure in 1921 the iron ore barges alongside the quay were left to rot, as shown here about 1926.   (Collection G. Freeston)

variations in detail between individual quarries. Gravity working, with horses to haul up the empties, was also sometimes used. Cable haulage throughout (ie not just on an incline) was employed in a few quarries eg Newbridge (1867) Finedonhill (1875) and Thingdon (1880).

The ore was sent away by railway in nearly every case, canals carrying but an insignificant fraction; the Grand Junction canal carried ore from Blisworth to Staffordshire in the 1860's and from Gayton to Stanton Ironworks near Ilkeston in 1867 (as recorded in Hewlett), and later between the Blisworth quarries and Hunsbury Hill Ironworks or for putting on rail at Blisworth station. Otherwise the only known lengthy haul of ore by canal was from Adderbury in Oxfordshire to ironworks in South Staffordshire, using the Oxford Canal; but this too gave way to rail transport. One of the first two ironstone tramways—Manor Farm, Wellingborough—ran to the LNWR but was in the 1870's diverted to a wharf on the River Nene; where, or indeed if, any ore was sent nobody knows.

Level crossings were fairly common, mostly on minor roads, but Wellingborough's metre gauge line crossed the busy Finedon Road, requiring a regular crossing keeper with a flag. Peckett 2029 snorts over the crossing on 24th March 1960 with empty wagons for the quarries. (S. A. Leloux)

The introduction of steam locomotive haulage is, like other matters, imperfectly recorded for these beginnings, but appears to have commenced on the standard gauge lines with longer hauls, as at Duston (1854) and Lodge Plantation (1869); on the narrow gauge the earliest known examples are Irchester (1872), Islip (1875) and Cransley (1877)—again, those with longer lines. From then on, the use of locomotives became general, new systems having them from the start and older ones being converted; but it was not a complete changeover—the Cottesmore quarries (1882) used horses for 40 years or more; Hunsbury Hill (1873) did not get steam locos until 1912, while Greetwell (1873) used horses throughout its life to the late 1930's, two experiments with locomotives proving unsuccessful. There was occasional use of horses on standard gauge lines, as at Tilton (1880). The standard gauge lines serving the quarries along the Grantham-Lincoln line were all laid and worked by the GNR, a unique arrangement as far as is known; it is just possible that it was applied elsewhere (eg Burton Latimer) without any record surviving, as there are indeed very few records about the GNR operations, which started about 1880.

One of the attractions of the ironstone tramways, particularly the narrow gauge, was the unobtrusive way they headed across the countryside, as on this section of the 3ft. gauge system at Islip, Northamptonshire. The track runs along the edge of the field from Willow Close Mine (behind camera, left) and Quarry (behind camera, right) to the main tramway running down the valley. The photo was taken in 1948 after abandonment of this section. (G. Foster Smith)

From about 1900 nearly all new quarries had standard gauge connections direct with the main line railways, the first major system being Buckminster (1898). Narrow gauge was only adopted in a few small systems or when special circumstances warranted it, eg in mines or in conjunction with aerial ropeways, where transhipment was inevitable in any case. Some narrow gauge systems were converted to standard gauge (Harringworth; Woolsthorpe), others to lorry transport (Eaton; Tilton; Eastwell; Cottesmore). In mines, horse haulage continued, but diesel locomotives were introduced at Wellingborough, Islip and Nettleton, and electric traction at the last and at Thistleton.

There was one aerial ropeway as far back as 1871 at Burton Dassett in Warwickshire, but the rest were all 20th century, including three from World War I (Lamport; Earls Barton; Eaton) followed by Nettleton (1930) and Rothwell Hill (1959). These installations were made where a simple narrow gauge incline was impracticable or, in the case of Rothwell Hill, in place of a difficult overland line.

One of the most photogenic of ironstone railways was undoubtedly the 3ft. gauge Kettering system. Here, in April 1961, a Manning Wardle locomotive rattles along with its train of wooden wagons bound for the furnaces. The minimal interference with the countryside is obvious.

(G. D. King)

The highly polished Peckett SCALDWELL with its train from Holcot Quarries approaches the bridge under Holcot Road in its way to the tipping dock at Scaldwell, Northamptonshire, July 1962. In the background is Pitsford Reservoir. This locomotive is now preserved at the Chalk Pits Museum, Sussex.

(G. P. Roberts)

61

The Eaton area of Leicestershire abounded in narrow gauge tramway interest, and this picture of Bagnall locomotive PIONEER at Eastwell on 8th June 1954 is typical. The two Bagnall six-wheelers were used mainly on the long-distance work, leaving the smaller four-wheelers to purely quarry duties.

(G. D. King)

Ironstone tramways, in the nature of things, were mostly on farm land, and sometimes invaded the farmyard itself. As here, at Eaton, Leicestershire, where a Ransome & Rapier 422 dragline stands ready to load the next train.
(The Farmer & Stockbreeder)

To the enthusiast there was always magic in approaching a locomotive shed, especially one in such delightful surroundings as Waltham, Leicestershire. The line on the right runs up to the tipping dock on the BR Eaton Branch, and to the right of the loco shed can be seen a wagon on the Branch. 8th March 1953.

(C. P. Knight)

Aerial ropeways offered an alternative to tramways, but their inherent shortcomings limited usage to special cases where difficult terrain was involved. Such was the case with the later example between Rothwell Hill and Corby, here shown where it crossed the road near Triangular Lodge, now a Listed Building.　　　(G. F. Barnes)

The standard gauge had the obvious advantage of allowing main line wagons to be loaded at the quarry face or calcining clamp and, as time went on, accorded with the use of larger loading machines; the production of iron ore was affected by the general trend in industry towards increased mechanisation and reduced hand labour. New rail systems with hills to climb did so by adhesion, with longer routes if necessary (Lamport; Exton Park; Harlaxton), the solitary example of a rope-worked incline at Edge Hill proving an economic failure.

The narrow gauge systems, however, were not by any means eliminated, but were developed and improved where appropriate, and several lasted into the 1960's, giving added colour to the scene for the enthusiast. The commonest gauge was 3ft., followed by 2ft. 6in. and metre; 2ft. was rare except in Oxfordshire. The 'odd' gauges were nearly all old tramways that had been built for horse operation before

65

Whilst the standard gauge lines could not compete on equal terms with the narrow gauge for pictorial appeal, their rural surroundings made them attractive. Bagnall locomotive LAMPORT No. 3 eases its train of loaded dumpcars from New Bridge Quarry near Hanging Houghton, Northamptonshire on 9th April 1961. This line replaced an earlier 3ft. gauge system running to an aerial ropeway.   (Ivo Peters)

(Opposite page) Glendon Quarries in Northamptonshire were the longest-lived in the ironstone industry, lasting 117 years. One of the Manning Wardles formerly at Corby emerges from the bridge under the A6003 road with a load of stone from Bridge Pit, 29th March 1960. The plantation in the background covers 'hill and dale' workings of the neighbouring Geddington Quarries system.   (G. D. King)

One does not think of Corby as one of the more photogenic systems—but it had its picturesque spots. On 3rd September 1968, 57 blasts its way from Priors Hall Quarry towards the ironworks. The cutting wall on the right now serves as part of the Weldon Bypass. (H. A. Gamble)

The Rutland quarries were mostly on the high ground to the east of the Vale of Catmose, and the loaded ore trains had to descend to the Vale by narrow gauge tramway with rope-worked inclines or by standard gauge lines with stiff banks. In this picture Barclay locomotive BERYL pushes a loaded train from Burley Quarries from the reversing point near Flint's Covert. (Eric Tonks)

The last ironstone quarry to be opened with its own rail system was Mill Hill Quarry in Leicestershire; but the beauty of the countryside is such that this is no less attractive than its forebears of a century ago. In this typical summer scene of 21st June 1960, Peckett 1952 starts to pull away as the loader has filled the last wagon.

(G. D. King)

On balance, the quarries north of the Welland were the more attractive scenically than those to the south. As a sample, a train hauled by one of the Barclay locomotives passes on its way from Cedar Hill Quarries on the Woolsthorpe system, Leicestershire, in September 1963. These were the most distant of the Woolsthorpe quarries.

(G. P. Roberts)

One of the last quarries to be opened up on the Corby rail system was at Oakley, to which was laid a lengthy overland line abounding in banks and earthworks. In our picture taken 22nd June 1961, 56, the first of its class, blasts its way up the bank from Little Oakley with 19 loaded tipplers. (J. L. Hobson)

The centrepiece of this photograph of 7th October 1964 at Market Overton, Rutland, is the Hunslet locomotive JUNO, built 1958; but we have included it to show the chaired track and lineside hedge, an unusual feature for an industrial line.

(Ivo Peters)

Locomotive sheds come in all sorts and conditions. The one at Desborough 'Co-op' pits in Northamptonshire had seen better days—and so had the track. This photograph was taken 8th December 1965 when the ore being dug was used for purposes other than making iron, and the train to BR usually only one wagon at a time.   (S. A. Leloux)

In pouring rain 64 (ex-BR D 9549) is on its way from Wakerley Quarries to Corby Works, 21st December 1979, within a few days of complete closure. Note the colour-light signal covering the approach to the single track under the Gretton road bridge; also the worked-out site of Brookfield East Quarry.   (J. Wade)

Level crossings were common on the quarry tramway systems, particularly where minor roads were involved; they made ideal spots for cameramen, as here at Byfield Quarries near the south Northamptonshire border. No. 3 AVONSIDE takes its train over the Byfield-Boddington lane on its way to the BR sidings on 7th August 1964. Not a car in sight!
(M. J. Leah)

While level crossings were common, the few lines alongside public roads were behind hedges. In our view of about 1970 Sentinel diesel BETTY brings its train from No. 7 Quarry, Harlaxon, Lincolnshire, towards the Swine Hill level crossing. On the right is Gorse Lane, looking towards Grantham. (J. Ginns)

Cranford was a typical Staveley locomotive shed of green corrugated iron, with the familiar row of 'pots' in the roof. There is a small workshop at the rear. In this picture, taken on 6th September 1967 during the midday break, a Bagnall locomotive is sizzling outside the shed, with two dumpcars on the siding next to the shed and coal wagons on the right; and a row of loaded tipplers on the BR siding at the rear.
(P. H. Groom)

Nassington Barrowden Mining Co Ltd. The shed building at Nassington, near Peterborough, was used only for repair work, with the locomotives standing outside; this picture of 28th March 1967 emphasises its rural setting. The locomotives are RING HAW (Hunslet) and BUCCLEUCH (Peckett) with a spare boiler; the other Hunslet, JACKS GREEN, was in the shed. The quaint name Ring Haw derives from the piece of woodland seen at the rear.

(G. D. King)

Ore brought up from the quarries in narrow gauge wagons usually had to be transferred to standard gauge wagons. The most common type of narrow gauge wagon was the side-tipper, and the picture shows a rake of 3ft. gauge wagons being emptied at Scaldwell Quarries, Northamptonshire. Note the chains to break up the larger lumps of ore. c.1960. (M. Winnett)

the days of standardisation. Early wagons were usually of wood, often with removable ends or sides for tipping or shovelling, and there was considerable diversity in transfer mechanisms at the tipping dock. The crudest was the laborious 'plate tippler' of early days, where the wagons or tubs were run one at a time on to a metal plate that was then levered up at a steep angle to discharge the load; an easier method was a simple platform, but with the wooden wagons fitted with bodies centrally pivoted so that they could be tipped sideways or forwards to release the load through hinged sides or ends. Then there were various forms of rotary tipplers, where the wagons were placed singly or in pairs in a cage or trunnions, that could be inverted over the railway wagon below. Standard gauge wagons were formerly supplied by the operator or by the ironworks, and varied according to the facilities at the latter; plank wagons or hoppers were the commonest. Since 1940 wagons have been standard 'pool' types, the

On many narrow gauge systems various forms of rotary tippler were employed, the wagons being run into a cage or box and overturned to empty their contents into a railway wagon below. This example is at Loddington Quarries, Northamptonshire in 1952. (G. H. Starmer)

commonest in BR days being the 27-ton Iron Ore Tippler.

Road transport of iron ore between quarry and works or railhead is as old as the industry itself, as Thomas Butlin used it at his East End Works in the 1850's, but was very little practised until modern times. The narrow gauge tramway was the preferred alternative for the smaller quarries, and road transport only used from quarries a long distance from any railhead (Shutlanger; Chelveston; Wothorpe; Great Tew) or where there were topographical difficulties (Cranford Hall; Hook Norton (Baker); Easton on the Hill); or, once, where direct shovelling into railway wagons was possible (Irchester Stanton). These were all horse-and-cart operations of course. Lorry transport began at the unlikely place of Midland Brick quarry, near Wellingborough Ironworks, and was used exclusively by Nassington-Barrowden Mining Co Ltd at their Barrowden and Rushton quarries, while Stewarts & Lloyds Minerals Ltd used lorries to replace the outmoded narrow gauge tramways at Eaton and Tilton. The most extensive use of lorries was planned for the quarries served by the BR High Dyke line, using special

Work in the quarries was never easy. Locomotives had to be coaled by hand, warm work on a summer's day. CARMARTHEN at Irchester, Northamptonshire on 9th September 1968. (P. H. Groom)

In the winter work was even harder. Buckminster in Lincolnshire was an exposed place and snow of this depth not uncommon. This 1957 view looks towards the level crossing with the road to Gunby, the crossing lying between the crane (left) and sheds (right).(F. Cooper)

In the quarries, rail tracks had to be slewed sideways fairly frequently, as the working faces were cut back. With the narrow gauge lines this had to be done the hard way, as shown here at Kettering on 18th January 1966.   (S. A. Leloux)

On the standard gauge lines the job was generally made easier by employing a 'Nordberg Trackshifter', seen here at work at Woolsthorpe Quarries, Leicestershire, April 1959.   (BSC)

One of the delights of the ironstone quarries was the ever-changing pattern of the railway system as exhausted areas were closed and new ones opened up. This was particularly noticeable when roads had to be crossed. Sometimes a level crossing would be put in, as at Buckminster No.16 ('School') Quarry in April 1963. When first opened the output from this quarry was sent a roundabout route via Sewstern, and then a cut off was made, saving two miles per trip. A loaded train at the shallow quarry face can be seen behind the hedge, with Ransomes & Rapier 480 dragline, and behind it, R & R W80 walking dragline. (BSC)

At other times, particularly when busier roads were involved, bridges were demanded, and our picture shows the rather attractive concrete bridge put under Gorse Lane to take the track to No. 4 ('Hungerton') Quarry, Harlaxton, Lincolnshire, in March 1958. Some ore was extracted in the process, as will be noted on the left. The water tower of the loco shed can be seen above the trees, left.   (BSC)

81

roads (Colsterworth; Sproxton); but this plan was never fully implemented, nor was S&LM's similar scheme at Barrowby (Harlaxton).

These were all in the eastern and northern parts of the ironstone field, but lorries were also used latterly at Twywell and Rothwell Hill in Northamptonshire. Had the industry survived, there is little doubt that the use of lorries between quarry and railhead would have become more widespread, but as things turned out they were never used in more than a subsidiary capacity. One side effect of these operations was that quarrying could be carried out in 'blocks' rather than the strips necessary when rail transport was used; and the surveyors' plans reveal clearly those areas where lorries were used.

Many of the narrow gauge ironstone tramways surviving World War II were replaced either by standard gauge lines or by road transport, as at Tilton, Leicestershire. Here, most of the output derived from the opposite side of the BR line, which was crossed by a Bailey bridge structure, the lorries using a modified tipping dock at the original site. Photo probably about 1955. (F. Cooper)

Had ironstone quarrying lasted longer, there is little doubt that there would have been considerable extension of the use of road vehicles to bring ore to a main line railhead. At Colsterworth, Lincolnshire, a 4 mile special roadway was built to open up the Ponton Heath area, but in fact it was never used for its intended purpose. Our picture shows a section of this deserted highway on October 10th 1979.   (Eric Tonks)

The narrow gauge steam locomotive — of almost any design — holds an extraordinary fascination. On the ironstone tramways there was plenty of variety, some of them of wellknown types, others less common. One of the latter is J. D. ELLIS, (Sharp Stewart 2298 of 1873) at Loddington Quarries, Northamptonshire. Of metre gauge, she has many features typical of her makers. A very crude 'cab' has been added, hardly improving her appearance but doubtless approved of by the driver.The Ellis family is also commemorated in 'Ellistown', a row of workmen's homes in the village. 13th September 1949. (F. Jones)

Locomotives

The vast majority of the locomotives used in the quarries were of the maker's standard designs, sometimes modified slightly to meet local requirements; but they came from a wide variety of makers and the many narrow gauge locomotives had the extra attractiveness of their kind. Only two types of locomotive are known to have been built specifically for ironstone work and represented nowhere else. One appeared in the 1880's — the four vertical-cylindered machines built by Staveley for their narrow gauge systems at Eastwell and Waltham, of which photographs fortunately survive to show what they were like;

Few ironstone locomotives were built specifically for their duties, but Islip had three of these unusual Kilmarnock Engineering locomotives for working their lengthy line to Slipton, with a restrictive tunnel. No. 6, shown here about 1950, sports a Ruston smokebox door—one of the innovations of Mr Purser, the engineer. (BSC)

a verbal description of these unusual engines would not have been very helpful, we feel! The other class unique to ironstone was the well-known '56 Class' supplied to Stewarts & Lloyds Minerals Ltd (nine at Corby and one at Harlaxton); these were built 1950-58 by Robert Stephenson & Hawthorns Ltd to a design worked out between builder and operator to incorporate the well-proven excellent features of their early Manning Wardle types in a machine on the modern lines set by the Hunslet 'Austerity' class and are described in the appropriate sections. The history of the Staveley locomotives required a lot of research by several people up and down the country—Chesterfield, Lincoln, Reading, Gainsborough—to establish their background! It is possible that some of the unknown locomotives which worked in the quarries in very early days were local products, but no records survive.

Hudswell Clarke products were well represented on the narrow gauge systems; LORD GRANBY (HC 633 of 1902) was one of the 3ft. gauge locomotives at Eastwell, Leicestershire, and, happily, is now preserved in Leeds Industrial Museum. This photograph of her on 30th June 1952 shows her at work. Lord Granby is the title of the Duke of Rutland's eldest son.

(K. Cooper/IRS Collection)

The two French Corpet locomotives were much photographed, deservedly so with the beautiful backdrop of the woods near High Leys, on the metre gauge quarry system at Waltham, Leicestershire on 25th July 1949.
(K. Cooper/IRS collection)

Another standard design — though even 'standard' locomotives in industry tended to acquire individual characteristics — was HARSTON (Bagnall 1587 of 1899) at Eaton Ropeway Quarries, Leicestershire, on 3rd September 1947. Note the highly-polished brass dome. The name derives from another quarry area owned by Stanton Ironworks Co Ltd.   (G. Alliez/courtesy B. D. Stoyel)

Manning Wardle locomotives had a reputation for rugged construction and a capacity for hard work under difficult conditions. MW 1795 of 1912 was at Irchester Quarries, Northamptonshire, and was photographed on 13th August 1965. Note the large cab and the ladder for filling the tank — the latter an embellishment to several South Durham Steel & Iron Co Ltd locomotives.   (P. H. Groom)

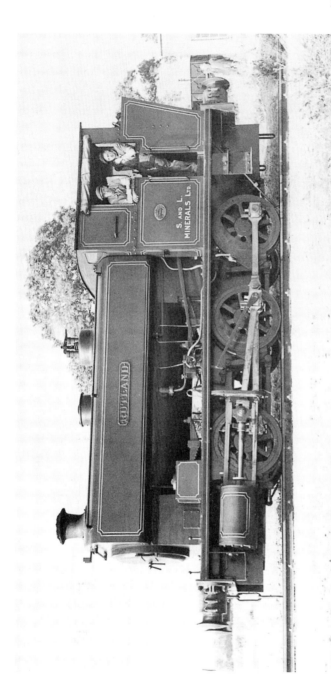

In the post World War II years Stanton Ironworks Co Ltd and their successors, Stewarts & Lloyds Minerals Ltd, standardised largely on Barclay locomotives with 15in. cylinders for their quarries north of the Welland. RUTLAND (AB 2351 of 1954) is one of them; she moved round quite a bit but is here shown at Buckminster in Lincolnshire on 23rd September 1954. The name has obvious local associations.

(G. Alliez/courtesy B. D. Stoyel)

The United Steel Cos Ltd owned a number of ironstone quarries in South Lincolnshire and Rutland and most of their locomotives were supplied by Yorkshire Engine Co Ltd, which belonged to United Steels. Shown is YE 2483 at Exton Park, Rutland, in the smart maroon livery adopted to replace the former apple green. In either livery, the locomotives were always kept spotless.(K. Cooper/IRS Collection)

Burley Quarries in Rutland were the only quarries in the Midlands owned by Dorman Long, owners of the vast iron and steel works in the North East. In the main the Burley locomotive stock derived from these works — hence the cutdown JUPITER (HL 2604 of 1906) and 33 (AB 1059 of 1905), photographed 11th May 1962 in leafy surroundings very different from their origins!

(Ivo Peters)

One of the few classes designed specifically for ironstone work was the '56' class built by Robert Stephenson & Hawthorns Ltd to Stewarts & Lloyds Minerals' specification, and incorporating features of the Manning Wardles that had given such fine service. ACHILLES, at Harlaxton, Lincolnshire, was the last steam locomotive built for ironstone traffic. This photograph, taken on 14th June 1965, epitomises the God of Strength. (K. Cooper/IRS Collection)

Opposite page
There were few diesel locomotives in the ironstone quarries on the narrow gauge, but more in the mines. The picture shows two Ruston & Hornsby 30 horsepower engines supplied to the 3ft. gauge system at Cottesmore, Rutland. The line to the right goes to the quarries, that to the left to the incline top, under the footpath bridge. Photograph taken 1935. (Ruston & Hornsby)

In all there were nearly 400 locomotives in the industry, about one third being of narrow gauge, with 0-4-0ST and 0-6-0ST predominating; as the lines became longer, the six-wheelers were preferred. With the different lines, generally well-kept condition and interesting names, the locomotives were always a source of delight to enthusiasts able to

obtain photographs with tree-lined backgrounds. It is pleasant to be able to record that many of them survive in preservation.

The ironstone quarries remained faithful to steam after most industrial systems had changed to diesel traction, with the last two steamers being supplied in 1958; Ruston & Hornsby narrow gauge locomotives were used in mines but on the long hauls then common on the quarry lines the diesels available at the time showed fewer advantages over steam than in purely shunting work. Oxfordshire Ironstone Co Ltd replaced their entire steam fleet by thirteen Sentinel diesels in the early 1960's, while Stewarts & Lloyds Minerals Ltd experimented with various Sentinel designs and one Yorkshire Engine, then bought 23 Swindon-built class 14 locomotives from BR. No other makers were represented in the quarries apart from trials.

Lorries arrived on the scene only in the last 40 years, but showed considerable changes from a few small 'Muir Hill' dumpers and conventional lorries with tip-up backs to the hefty purpose-built Aveling Barford machines of the 1960's.

Electric locomotives were confined to mines, as far as the ironstone industry was concerned — Irthlingborough (Northamptonshire), Nettleton and Thistleton (Lincolnshire). At Irthlingborough were trolley locomotives such as the Greenwood & Batley machine shown, on 7th June 1958. These brought the mine cars out to the sinter plant, while small battery locomotives worked at the underground galleries. In later years the trolley locomotives were converted to battery operation in compliance with revised legislation.   (J. A. Peden)

The ironstone quarries were still buying steam locomotives up to 1958, as a result of which very few diesels were used, and those of modern design in general. Shown is a Sentinel 'Steelman' working at Glendon Quarries, Northamptonshire on 23rd July 1974. A very sophisticated machine with independent springing to the wheels and other refinements.

(N. L. Cadge)

Most of the diesel locomotives in the ironstone quarries were either 'Sentinels' or ex-BR Class D95XX built at Swindon, and little used by BR because of changing traffic patterns. In all, Stewarts & Lloyds Minerals Ltd purchased 23 of these in 1968. Harlaxton and Buckminster quarries in Lincolnshire were completely dieselised, using this class on trains to the main line. Those at Harlaxton had the cab roofs lowered to negotiate a low bridge under Gorse Lane. Shown here is ex-BR D9548 in Harlaxton sidings. 6th July 1970.(N. L. Cadge)

The use of lorries commenced in 1940 mainly to replace small narrow gauge railways at first. Usage on a much larger scale would certainly have come about had the industry lasted longer. The photograph in October 1960 shows two AEC types—the conventional lorry and the more sophisticated 'dumptruck'. Photograph probably taken in the Eaton area.

(BSC)

97

Lorry operation at Hurst's South Pit, Eaton, Leicestershire. The work here, with fairly shallow overburden, required only simple equipment — a 22RB dragline and lorries. No track slewing necessary! But lacking the pictorial charm of the narrow gauge tramways. (BSC)

Quarry Machines

The first machines in the ironstone quarries were introduced by Lloyds Ironstone Co Ltd at Corby from 1895 and were supplied by John H. Wilson & Co Ltd of Liverpool. Lloyds used the first machine for loading ironstone but very soon started to use machines for the more important task of removing overburden that in some Lloyds quarries exceeded the 25ft. generally regarded as the practicable limit of hand labour. The main problem lay in dealing with the material dug up and much effort was put into this by Wilsons and by A. R. Grosssmith, Lloyd's engineer at the time. Various forms of conveyor were devised—some of them distinctly weird looking contraptions—and in 1899 came the first long-jib navvy; from these experiments the transporter or conveyor emerged as the most satisfactory answer and various forms of these were devised including combined excavator and

The early quarry machines were the steam navvies; shown here is a typical set-up at one of Stanton's quarries (probably Woolsthorpe, Leicestershire), with a shovel digging ironstone for loading into narrow gauge tubs. Another machine can be seen in the next field. (BSC)

A No. 12 Ruston steam shovel on rails loading calcine at Irchester Quarries,
Northamptonshire, about 1933. Irchester had a large fleet of steam quarrying
equipment.   (Collection B. Smith)

The largest steam machine in the ironstone fields was the No. 300 Ruston & Hornsby long-jib stripping shovel, originally supplied to Irchester Quarries but later moved to the South Durham Steel and Iron Co Ltd quarries at Storefield, Northamptonshire. She is here photographed at work on 26th April 1962. The size of this monster is well shown by the men standing in front of her, and by the standard gauge railway wagons and the small 43RB diesel loading shovel.

(G. H. Starmer)

101

transporters, first by Whitaker Bros Ltd of Leeds (examples at Storefield, Loddington and Glendon) and then by Ruston Proctor & Co Ltd of Lincoln.

Alfred Hickman's quarries at Astrop, near Banbury, had a long-jib Wilson machine, rather surprising for so small a quarry, but it was not until World War I that the use of machines became widespread, because of the availability of financial assistance from the Ministry of Munitions, who were anxious to expedite production of the extra iron ore required for armaments, and to release men for the Services. The order books of Ruston Proctor show this dramatically; in 1914-18 over half their excavator production was for ironstone. Ruston Proctor of Lincoln was the principal manufacturer of these steam-operated machines, having shortly before World War I acquired this side of the business of Whitaker Bros Ltd of Leeds. Machines also came from a few other manufacturers, including some 'Railway Type' with long frames and rail wheels, imported from the USA, of which Lloyds Ironstone had some and also Oxfordshire Ironstone (Bucyrus and Marion).

Ruston & Proctor's innovations for the wartime period included the bucket door controlled by the driver and the 'combined navvy and grab' that enabled the same long-jib No. 20 machine to perform as a shovel for digging the ironstone and for stripping overburden by susbstituting the grab for the bucket. The removal of overburden soon, however, became the province of the draglines, the first example of which came from the Bucyrus Co in America in the second half of World War I, with examples at Wakerley (another surprise ...) and at Buckminster, followed by larger machines at Corby and Cranford.

The story of quarry machines was entirely different from that of locomotives, which changed little in essentials and only the '56 Class' can be said to have been influenced by ironstone quarry practice. Development of quarry machines was continual and was certainly influenced by the problems peculiar to the ironstone industry, particularly as deeper quarrying was made possible by the introduction of more powerful and versatile machines. On the locomotive side, steam was not displaced until the 1960's; but petrol-paraffin machines appeared in the late 1920's and diesels and electrics in the 1930's, when few steam were built. By then the market was dominated by Ruston-Bucyrus Ltd (formed in 1930 from a fusion of the interests of Ruston & Hornsby in this field with the Bucyrus Erie Co of America) and Ransomes & Rapier Ltd of Ipswich, who supplied their first ironstone machine in 1929.

In order to deposit the overburden further away from the railway tracks, long-jib shovels were introduced, then transporters or conveyors of various types. The picture shows a Ruston No. 18 steam shovel and a No. 5 transporter at Sudborough Quarry, Islip, Northamptonshire on 26th May 1945. The carrier is nearing the top of the conveyor and after depositing its load will return to the shovel for a refill.

(B.G.S.)

The success of the shovel/transporter team led to the designing of machines combining both functions. This example at Loddington Quarries, Northamptonshire, was built in 1909 by Whitaker Bros of Leeds. There were several variants of this type of machine, but they all looked rather clumsy!

(Collection B. Smith)

The complete steam system at Cherry Hill Quarry, Glendon, Northamptonshire, in 1934. At the rear a No. 20 Ruston shovel digs the overburden for the No. 5 transporter to dump on the worked-out ground, while in the foreground another No. 20 shovel loads hopper wagons.   (BSC (copied G. H. Starmer))

From the early 1930's Ruston-Bucyrus offered a range of machines from 10 to 100 tons, shovels and draglines; the diesels predominated at first, as few quarries had the necessary power laid on, delivery of electric machines commencing in the later 1930's, but overall diesels outnumbered electrics 2:1. This range was widened a little in succeeding decades and there were design changes; but the most important advance was the introduction of the walking dragline which so greatly simplified movement along the quarry; the first 5W was delivered to Wellingborough quarries in 1940.

Ransomes & Rapier offered a range of machines generally similar in capacity but overall they concentrated on the larger stuff, starting off with the famous 5360 Stripping Shovel; these handsome machines were familiar in many of the big quarries right to the end. R&R also built walking draglines parallel with RB, but R&R built more electrics

While on the locomotive side the quarry companies remained faithful to steam later than most industries, the change from steam to diesel or electric quarry machines took place mostly in the 1930's. The photograph shows a Ruston Bucyrus 43RB diesel dragline with a long (70ft.) boom depositing overburden at Hurst's Pit, Eaton, Leicestershire, in July 1938, well beyond the narrow gauge wagons at the ironstone face. (BSC)

The most popular loading shovel was the Ruston Bucyrus 100RB, either diesel or electric powered. Shown here is an electric machine (as indicated by the cables), at Bridge Pit, Glendon, Northamptonshire, loading into hopper wagons, which were commonly used. The machine is on caterpillar tracks. (Ruston Bucyrus)

Wroxton Quarries. Loading dumpcars at Balscott Quarry, 7th September 1959. Machine is a Ruston Bucyrus 100RB electric shovel. (J. A. Peden)

One of the best-known machines designed to deal with heavier overburden was the Ransomes & Rapier 5360 class of Electric Stripping Shovel. They were handsome machines, dominating the quarries where they worked, and did many years of hard daily work. Shown is R&R 1163 at Bridge Pit, Glendon, Northamptonshire, on 25th May 1945, with a small shovel alongside the ironstone face, loading skip wagons. The overburden here is 23ft. but became deeper later on. (B.G.S.)

(Opposite page) The Ruston Bucyrus machine, the 5W Electric Walking Dragline, is here shown at Geddington Pit, Glendon, Northamptonshire, on 22nd June 1948.(BSC)

Movement of large machines along the quarry floor was a tedious business that was largely overcome by the development of the 'Walking Dragline', which 'walked' on two large feet. Ruston Bucyrus and Ransomes & Rapier both designed machines of this type, and shown here is R&R's W90 at Denton Park Quarry, Woolsthorpe, Leicestershire in June 1964. (BSC)

The ultimate in quarrying machines, and the best-known, were the 'big machines' at Corby; the first came from America, but the others were built by Ransomes & Rapier Ltd, designed in conjunction with Stewarts & Lloyds Ltd. Their large size makes it difficult to obtain a photograph that adequately conveys the scene. This view at Priors Hall Quarry about 1957 shows the W1400 at work, with a 100RB shovel digging up ironstone that has been loosened by explosives. This W1400 has a 282ft. boom.

(BSC/R. Sismey)

When the early Barn Close Quarry at Corby was reopened, the W1400 Electric Walking Dragline was moved here over the road from Cowthick Quarry in 1971. She has the longest boom of them all — 303ft. She was the last to go, being cut up in 1987. In the foreground is a permanent way train. (S. A. Leloux)

than diesels, in line with the tendency for smaller machines to be diesel, the larger electric.

As overburdens deepened beyond the range of existing plant, recourse was had to doing the job in two operations, but this cumbersome method was overcome by the introduction of the famous 'Big Machines'; the first, at Brookfield Cottage Quarry, Corby, came from Bucyrus Erie, then Stewarts & Lloyds Ltd collaborated with Ransomes & Rapier Ltd in designing a large dragline specifically for the ironstone quarries, and four were built for the East Midlands, three

The big machines had to be dismantled for movement. Here the jib of the 5360 shovel is being taken down from Buccleuch Quarry, Finedon, Northamptonshire, for re-erection at Blisworth. The quarry locomotives had been disposed of by then (about 1954) and 51235 was hired from BR to do the job. (Richard Thomas and Baldwins)

W 1400s and one W 1800, all latterly at Corby. A W 2000 was on order when the ironstone industry collapsed. These colossal and awe-inspiring machines had a beauty of their own, very successfully drawing attention away from the devastation of the countryside surrounding them.

More detailed information on quarry machines is contained in the excellent series of papers by W. Barnes under the title *'Excavating Machinery in the Ironstone Fields'* published in 'The Engineer' for 7, 14, 21 and 28 August 1942; this is the most complete account of the subject from the historical and mechanical points of view. *'Introduction to Excavating Practice'* by A. H. Wade (brochure issued by Ruston-Bucyrus Ltd 1957) continues the story, including information from other manufacturers; while the 'Big Machines' are best described in the

Sometimes it was expedient to put the rail track on top of the ironstone face instead of alongside. In the upper picture a No. 20 Ruston navvy loads wagons at Cranford Quarries, Northamptonshire. The lower picture shows a later operation, with the machine on a level with the rail track. An early Ruston Bucyrus 100RB dragline loads hopper wagons at No. 10 Quarry, Buckminster, Lincolnshire in 1940.

(Upper—Ruston Bucyrus. Lower—BSC)

Movement of quarry machines was never easy and always slow. Here a 480 Ransomes & Rapier dragline crosses Stainby Sidings, Lincolnshire, on its caterpillar track.

(F. Cooper)

brochure produced by Stewarts & Lloyds Minerals Ltd as *'The Great Walking Draglines of Corby'*.

In addition to the excavating plant, the quarry operators used a whole battery of other machines for drilling etc, and earth-moving, particularly on restoration work; but we have confined our attention to those essentially concerned with iron ore production.

115

Restoration

In early leases for ironstone extraction there was usually a clause requiring the operator to restore the land to agricultural use, a task presenting no great difficulty where the overburden was shallow (examples—Kettering; Caythorpe; Wartnaby). Problems began to arise as quarrying became progressively deeper, a factor recognised in the framing of new leases, when the lessee had the option of paying the lessor an agreed sum in respect of land that it was economically impracticable to restore completely. Sometimes such areas were planted with trees, but others were simply left in the derelict state (examples—Finedon; Whiston; Storefield (with trees); Gretton (with trees); Wakerley; Greetwell; Fawler; Hook Norton; Edge Hill). This position was severely aggravated by mechanical stripping, where the

One of the effects of using machines was the deposition of overburden in long rows parallel to the working face to form the familiar 'hill and dale' pattern, well shown in this view of Colsterworth North Quarry, 23rd September 1972. Before the days of obligatory restoration, some areas were left in this condition. In the foreground the Yorkshire Engine 200hp diesel locomotive takes its load to the BR sidings.

R. K. Hateley)

This aerial view of Irchester shows dramatically the phenomenon of 'hill and dale'. In the foreground is Wembley Pit, with the final face adjacent to Gipsy Lane, with Lodge Pit still being worked beyond (note the 5360 machine). It was large scale devastation of this kind, especially in Northamptonshire, that led to the introduction of legislation making restoration obligatory from 1951. In many quarries, like Wembley, that were closed before then, afforestation with conifers made some use of the ground. This view was taken about 1950.

shovel travelling along the working face dumped the spoil in a parallel ridge behind it to form the familiar feature of 'hill and dale'. By the late 1930's as such machines became more common and the workings deeper, the increasing unsightly areas aroused concern locally and nationally, resulting in the setting up by the Government in 1938 of a committee chaired by Lord Kennet to examine the problem and make recommendations. Mainly because of the outbreak of World War II, no action was then taken, but in 1944 a further committee under Mr A. H. Waters was appointed to take up the matter.

Comprehensive legislation arising from these beginnings took two forms. Under the Town & Country Planning Act, 1947, local planning authorities (usually the county councils) were given power to allocate iron ore-bearing land for future needs, while current developments were covered by 'The Ironstone Areas Special Development Order' (S.I. 1177 of 1950), which provided for the levelling of all such workings after 1st April 1951. Applications for working fresh areas for ironstone were to be referred to the Minister of Housing & Local Government for decision. The latter also controlled the fund, set up under the Mineral Workings Act, that came into force in 1951, to provide for restoration of opencast ironstone quarries. The fund was financed by the payment of 3d per statute ton in respect of all ironstone extracted by opencast methods, 2¼d being paid by the operator and ¾d by the Exchequer, but the former was empowered to recoup half his contribution from royalty payments under leases, so that in effect the operator paid 1⅛d, the landowner 1⅛d and the Exchequer ¾d. From 1st April 1951 all current workings were required to be restored, while areas that had previously been left in the rough condition, where the operators had made payment to the owner in lieu of restoration, could be similarly treated under direction of the local authority, who would be reimbursed from the Ironstone Restoration Fund.

The guiding principle was that the land should be restored in a way that would facilitate natural drainage and the resumption of normal agricultural work, including movement of machines; but practical considerations permitted some flexibility — for example, in some early applications under the Act, time limits for restoration were imposed but experience showed that better results were obtained by delaying operations until a larger area could be dealt with. The process of restoration was greatly affected by the depth of overburden and the character of the overlying strata, the deposited heaps of which had to be levelled off and the topsoil replaced; as the depth of quarrying

Irchester Quarries in Northamptonshire had the 'Colonel Stephens' approach; they mostly had to be content with secondhand locomotives and rarely scrapped one, but left them lying around the premises for years, with parts removed to keep others going. In this picture of 14th June 1962 are two Pecketts, ROTHWELL (left) and PROGRESS (right), with a row of 'Ship Canal' wagons. At the rear will be noted the conifer plantation covering the 'hill and dale' of Wembley Pit.

(S. A. Leloux)

Many quarries in the 1960's and 1970's had to record 'last day of operation'—always with sadness and with varying ways of marking the occasion. At Harlaxton, Lincolnshire, a special effort was made to record the event by the Press, as this was the final load of ore from north of the Welland. On an easily remembered date, St. Valentine's Day, 14th February 1974, Sentinel locomotive BETTY leaves the battery of machines at No. 4 Quarry with a load of ore for the last time.   (J. Ginns)

increased the complexity of restoring procedures was reflected in the number of machines required. Deep overburden often contained a thick layer of limestone, the disposition of which could be altered to give better conditions for drainage and crop-growing; and in some cases it was found desirable to change farming operations from arable to grazing land. Plantations of conifers were also made sometimes, even on land other than 'hill and dale'. With the ground restored, field boundaries were replaced, sometimes not precisely on their original alignment. In the past, hawthorn hedges were the commonest replacement, occasionally with spaced trees; at other times wooden fences were used but the commonest method in later years was

Wroxton Quarries. Locomotives in store following dieselisation, 28th March 1965. Though fascinating to the enthusiast, such a line of rusting derelicts was apt to invite criticism from an environmental viewpoint.

After replacement of the narrow gauge tramway by lorries, the locomotives and rolling stock at Eastwell, Leicestershire, were collected in the yard at the head of the incline to await the attention of 'Eric the Burner'. From left to right are UNDERBANK, THE SCOT, MOUNTAINEER, PIONEER, BELVOIR, on 28th June 1960. The locomotive shed can be glimpsed under the bridge. (P. Lynch)

The metre gauge Waltham Quarries system awaited its fate on 28th June 1960. One of the star attractions for locomotive enthusiasts was THE BARONET, Markham 102 of 1889, here lying out of use beyond the tippler, with the tree-lined Belvoir escarpment as backdrop. (M. C. Fayers)

An all too familiar sight from the 1950s onwards. Track lifting at Kettering Quarries, 26th November 1962. (S. A. Leloux)

hawthorn ('quicks') protected with wire fences to prevent damage by cattle.

The effect of the 1951 Act was that all ironstone workings from that date were restored after extraction was completed, whereas ground exhausted before that varied in condition according to the terms of the lease, some being fully restored, some left in the rough condition, while 'hill and dale' was usually planted with trees as the only practicable way of utilising the otherwise derelict land. A lot of these old areas have since been restored by local authorities and/or landowners under the terms of the Act, the last before the Ironstone Restoration Fund was wound up on 1st April 1985 being a portion of tramway cutting at Loddington.

It follows that the industrial archaeologist will often find more recognisable traces at the early quarry sites than the later ones, which modern earth-moving equipment has very effectively erased. An

Aerial views often reveal features not readily visible on the ground. The course of the Loddington tramway in Northamptonshire is visible in the centre of the picture, with gullets at the north end, while nearer on the ground are marks showing something of the pattern of quarrying. (J. R. Billows)

Ironstone mines (as distinct from quarries) were not far from the surface, and when they were closed their location was sometimes revealed by 'sink holes' where the surface had collapsed. Probably the most noted of these were the former Clay Cross mines at Cranford, Northamptonshire, photographed 24th March 1960. Most of these areas have now been filled in and levelled, but sections of the Cranford site are still severely cratered, but cloaked in heavy undergrowth. (S. A. Leloux)

The light covering of snow clearly etches the formation of the former rope-worked incline from Wartnaby Quarries, Leicestershire, to BR at Old Dalby. 23rd February 1969.   (P. D. Rowbotham)

interesting example is at Brixworth, where Clay Cross Co Ltd operated an area surrounded by the activities of Staveley Iron & Coal Co Ltd (a fine instance, incidentally, of the competition among ironmasters for prime ore sites); Clay Cross ceased in 1947 under leases that provided for payment in lieu of restoration, while Staveley carried on until 1963, with the obligation of full restoration. The contrast is very plain to see in the plenteous remains of the old Clay Cross Brixworth site even though in recent years more bits have been filled in or put under the plough, while traces of Staveley's Lamport quarries are few and far between—little more than a few bridge parapets and the office area at Scaldwell.

The most obvious signs of former quarrying areas is the lowering of the ground level by perhaps 10ft., which shows up well at boundary hedges alongside roads; the next best clue is afforded by the

Upon closure, the equipment at most quarries was completely dismantled and the ground restored according to the terms of the lease. These conditions did not apply at Easton on the Hill, near Stamford, where, apart from lifting of the tramway and disposal of the rolling stock, was left much as at the end of work. The tippler hods were indeed in position a few years before this picture was taken on 10th January 1976.

(J. Scholes)

replacement field boundaries of fences or hedges, which are of a uniformity out of keeping with ancient hedges. A rough rule for estimating the age of a hedge is to count the number of species of tree or shrub in a 30 yard length, within which one species is naturally added, on average, every century. Hawthorn is the most common type of replacement and the first intrusive tree almost invariably elder. Most such hedges on ironstone should contain no more, though some of the very early ones are coming up for a second invader now! Very often the boundaries of leased land coincided with parish boundaries—sometimes with one operator one side and another on the other; parish boundary hedges were usually left in any case, and the contrast in variety of species between these and replacement

While restoration was obligatory from 1950 onwards, quarries closed before then were sometimes left unrestored. The quarries thus left often became havens for wildlife, but mines were potentially dangerous. Our picture shows two adits of Thingdon Mines, Finedon, Northamptonshire, (Thingdon is the old spelling of Finedon). It was these that caused a local uproar when two children wandered in and were lost for a day or so in the underground labyrinth. They were rescued, but all such adits were then adequately filled in. Photo dated 24th May 1945.   (B.G.S.)

hedges is very marked. Apart from the hedges and the lowered levels, the different colour of the land will often reveal the site of quarrying, particularly deep workings; the contours are smoother and the soil and usage different from surrounding areas.

Nearly all quarries were served by tramways, of which the industrial archaeologist will usually be able to find traces, in the parapets of bridges, cuttings, embankments etc., this again applying more forcibly to pre-1951 restoration; for instance, in early abandonments, bridges

The vast majority of quarrying took place on land leased from the landowner for a specific period, and it sometimes happened that two different operators would be working adjacent fields. In such cases it was normal to leave the intervening hedge intact, especially if this had the special significance of a parish boundary. One example is shown here, where R. B. Sparrow worked the field to the left in Cayton parish, while P. Phipps worked that to the right, in Blisworth parish. About 1960.   (G. Freeston)

were frequently left open, but very few have been in recent years. The extensive Corby system has been almost entirely eradicated and the searcher for, say, the site of Harringworth Sidings will have some

Tramways crossing open fields seldom left much to identify the route, which the plough soon incorporated into the rest of the field. Routes through woodland were spared this form of destruction, as here illustrated on 27th April 1963 by the cutting through Hunsbury Hill spinney by the narrow gauge line. (S. A. Leloux)

Modern earth-moving techniques and long experience now enable operators to make a very thorough job of restoration of former quarry sites. This view of part of No. 4 Quarry, Harlaxton, Lincolnshire, in October 1970 is a fair example. The ground is completely levelled and the soil ready for planting — a bit stony maybe, but even that will improve with time. On the left men are replacing a former hedge by a wire fence. Not an ideal landscape, perhaps, but at least the ground has been restored to use. (BSC)

A group of Industrial Railway Society members walk the trackbed of the former Buckminster line in Lincolnshire, going north from Mill Lane, on 20th April 1986.   (A. Cocklin)

Two ironstone quarry sites have been designated Country Parks. Our view of October 19th 1985 is in Irchester Country Park, Northamptonshire, showing in the centre the deep final gullet of the Wembley Pit, with conifer plantations on the worked-out area to the left.
(A. Cocklin)

All that is left for the researcher on the ground are, in many cases, railway trackbeds.
An Industrial Railway Society party discusses the former Harlaxton line, Lincolnshire,
framed in the bridge under the Grantham road, 18th October 1986.   (A. Cocklin)

difficulty in assuring himself that he is on the right spot, or even in believing a marshalling yard could ever have existed; at Wroxton, on the other hand, though the quarries are now under cultivation, there is plenty to see and the four-mile trackbed to the main line is still mostly intact. No two cases are alike and the searcher after traces will at the very least be rewarded by a pleasant country walk. Abandoned quarries and tramway cuttings became havens for wildlife and flowers in a time of increasingly commercialised land usage, a factor belatedly recognised in the designation of some tracts as Conservation Areas (Finedon; Holwell; Wroxton), while Irchester and Burton Dassett have become Country Parks.

For a detailed account of restoration, readers should consult the paper *'Restoration of Ironstone Workings in the Midlands of Great Britain'* by T. W. Jones (Northern Area Chief Surveyor, Stewarts & Lloyds Minerals Ltd), printed in the Proceedings of the Symposium on Opencast Mining, Quarrying and Alluvial Mining arranged by the Institute of Mining and Metallurgy, 16-19th November 1964.

Ironstone Folklore

Ironstone quarrying, as we understand it, only goes back to 1851 and so has no deep roots in history; but in its 130 years a number of terms came to be used that, while not necessarily restricted to ironstone, are generally associated with it; and as they will in any case rapidly disappear from everyday usage, we have selected a few for mention. They appear in the main text where appropriate, but this is an opportunity to bring them together for the benefit of students of language.

Not surprisingly, most of them derive from the early days of universal hand labour—and it was hard work, too. Quarrymen usually started at 6 or 7 am and worked through to 3 or 4 pm; but as they came from surrounding villages, they often had some miles to walk to and from work, rain or shine. We now look at their labours through a sentimental haze, but it **was** a hard life, yet they seem to have accepted it cheerfully and have been happy to pass on their memories.

The time-honoured method of removing overburden by 'plank and barrow' was called—with neat disregard for philology—'baring' or 'unbaring', and the men so employed were 'toppers' in Oxfordshire, 'muckshifters' in Northamptonshire. The hazardous part of their job was 'running the plank' or 'top road running', and the trestles were often called 'trussells'.

Tramway operation was part and parcel of quarry work and gave rise to one term that is mostly associated with ironstone—the 'rope runner'. His duties were those of a 'shunter' and he was responsible for clipping wagons to the rope when cable haulage was involved, mostly on inclines; he thus became the 'rope runner' and the term came to be applied to 'shunters' generally even when only straightforward coupling was required, as on the standard gauge lines. We have seen the term used in official correspondence, so it was generally accepted. At the foot of rope-worked inclines, wagons detached from the rope were usually brought to rest by having a bar of hard wood or iron thrust into the spokes; this was called a 'sprag' and the operator would be nicknamed 'Sprag' too. This was a term used generally on industrial tramways. The early narrow gauge wagons were unsprung, and crude lubrication took the form of having a dollop of grease slapped over the axles—a process known as 'fatting the wagons'. At Eastwell wagons were sometimes referred to as 'corves' but this was not a term in general use.

A job associated with early loading shovels was that of opening the bucket door, the province of the 'rope puller'; this fell into disuse as mechanical control of bucket doors became general. Fixed-jib machines deposited overburden in long rows parallel to the travel of the machine along the working faces, giving rise to the pattern of 'hill and dale' on worked-out land, which was primarily responsible for the demand for compulsory restoration.

Aerial ropeways were few but had their own specialists in the form of 'shiners' who were responsible for oiling the cable from a travelling cradle, and 'pokers' who cleared the chutes loading the buckets.

Mining probably had its named jobs too, but we have not heard them specifically mentioned; mining was only carried out from adits by the method known as 'pillar and stall', with pillars of stone left in to support the roof; 'stoops and room' was an alternative phrase. Towards the end of operations 'pillar robbing' often took place, leading to irregular collapse of the surface in 'sink holes'.

The above list is only a brief review of the language of the quarrymen, and we confess to having neglected this aspect of the industry; we were so busy noting down what was to be seen and asking questions that we often overlooked the way in which we were answered. We hope that others may be able to find out more from old quarrymen while they are still around.

Chronology of Quarries

The table lists the quarry systems in order of opening by years; in each year the order adopted is by county—Northamptonshire, Rutland, Lincolnshire, Leicestershire, Oxfordshire, Warwickshire. The following points should be noted:-

Year of Opening and **Year of Closure.**
These are the years of commencement and cessation of production. In cases of uncertainty, the dates are given, for example, as c.1880.

Name of Quarry.
As in the main text, with identifying ownership where necessary.

County.
N=Northamptonshire; R=Rutland; Li=Lincolnshire; Le=Leicestershire; O=Oxfordshire; W=Warwickshire.

Transport System.
A separate line is used to indicate successive changes in any aspect of the quarry system in columns 4, 5 and 6. Thus:-
1855 Lodge Plantation. Narrow gauge horse-operated tramway to the canal was replaced by locomotive operation; this in turn was replaced by a standard gauge locomotive-worked tramway to the LNWR.
1898 Rothwell Hill. A combination of narrow gauge locomotive and cable haulage, including an incline, to the MR was replaced later by a combination of road (lorry) haulage and aerial ropeway to Corby Works. Abbreviations used:-

NG	Narrow gauge tramway
SG	Standard gauge tramway
H	Horse haulage
L	Locomotive haulage
C	Cable haulage
ML	Main line locomotive haulage (applies to Grantham-Lincoln line only)
Rd	Road haulage by cart or lorry
AeR	Aerial Ropeway

Special Features

> I=cable-worked incline.
> K=calcining kilns used
> M=Mines, sometimes in addition to Quarries

Main Line Connection or Terminus.

The usual abbreviations for main line railways are used; when the output went exclusively to an ironworks on site, this is given, otherwise the rail outlet is quoted.

Year of Opening	Name of Quarry	County	Transport System	Special F'tures	Main Line Connection or Terminus	Year of Closure
1851	Hardingstone	N	NG/SG	I	LNWR Blisworth-Peterborough	185X
1851/2	Manor Farm	N	NG		LNWR Blisworth-Peterborough	1855?
1852	Blisworth (Clare)	N	Rd(?)		Grand Junction Canal	1852
1852	Blisworth (Hickman/Bevan/Phipps)	N	NGH	I	Grand Junction Canal	1921
1853	Gayton (Hickman/Sparrow)	N	NGH/SGL	I	LNWR Northampton-Rugby	1921
			NGL		SMJ Blisworth-Towcester	
1853	East End	N	NGH/Rd		East End Ironworks, Wellingborough	1876
1855	Duston	N	SGL		LNWR Blisworth-Peterborough	1908
1855	Lodge Plantation	N	NGH		Grand Junction Canal	1878
			NGL		Grand Junction Canal	
1858	Cogenhoe	N	SGL		LNWR Northampton-Rugby	1888
			NGH/SGL	I.M	LNWR Blisworth-Peterborough	
1858	Wothorpe	N	Rd		-	1861
1858	Orton (nr. Peterborough)	N	-		-	1858
1859	Dallington (Wheldon)	N	-		LNWR Northampton-Market Harborough	1859
1859	Dallington (Bevan)	N	SG(?)/H		LNWR Northampton-Rugby	1863
1859	Desborough (Hickman)	N	NG or Rd.		MR Bedford-Leicester	1862
1859	Adderbury (Railton)	O	NG		Oxford Canal	c.1870
1859	Fawler	O	NGH	M	OWWR Oxford-Kingham	1885
1861	Nevill Holt	Le	NG/SG	I	LNWR Rugby-Peterborough	1874
1863	Gayton (Wheldon)	N	NG	I	SMJ Blisworth-Towcester	1884

Year of Opening	Name of Quarry	County	Transport System	Special F'tures	Main Line Connection or Terminus	Year of Closure
1863	Heyford	N	NG?	I	LNWR Northampton-Rugby	1868
1863	Brixworth (Watkins)	N	NG?	I	LNWR Northampton-Market Harborough	1874?
1863	Irthlingborough (Butlins)	N	SGL		(LNWR Blisworth-Peterborough	1921
					(MR Bedford-Leicester	
1866	Finedon (Glendon-Barlow-RT)	N	SGL		Finedon Ironworks	
			NGL/SGL		MR Bedford-Leicester	
			SGL		LMSR Bedford-Leicester	1946
1866	Woodford	N	NGH/SGL	M	MR Kettering-Cambridge	
			NGL/SGL		MR Kettering-Cambridge	1896
1867	Dean & Chapter	N	NG		River Nene	1878
			SGL		Irthlingborough Ironworks	
1867	Newbridge	N	NGC		MR Kettering-Cambridge	1892
1867	Islip	N	NGH		MR Kettering-Cambridge	
			NGL/H	M	Islip Ironworks	
			NGL/SGL	M	LMSR Kettering-Cambridge	1953
1868	Acre House	Li	NG	I.M	MSLR Claxby Branch	1885
1868	Burton Dassett	W	Rd		GWR Oxford-Leamington	
			NGH/AeR		SMJ Fenny Compton-Stratford	1925
c.1869	Adderbury	O	NGL		GWR Oxford-Leamington	
					Oxford Canal	c.1901
1870	Nell Bridge	N	NG		GWR Oxford-Leamington	1874

Year of Opening	Name of Quarry	County	Transport System	Special F'tures	Main Line Connection or Terminus	Year of Closure
1870	Aynho	N	Rd?		GWR Oxford-Leamington?	1874
c.1870	Blisworth (Bevan)	N	NGH		Grand Junction Canal	1902
c.1870	Cranford Hall	N	Rd.		MR Kettering-Cambridge	c.1874
1871	Ringstead (Butlins)	N	NG		LNWR Blisworth-Peterborough	1891
1871	Kettering	N	NG		MR Bedford-Leicester	
			NGL		Kettering Ironworks	
1872	Irchester	N	NGL/SGL		BR Bedford-Leicester	1962
			NGL		MR Bedford-Leicester	
			SGL		MR Bedford-Leicester	c.1878
1873	Shutlanger	N	Rd.		SMJ Blisworth-Towcester?	1874
1873	Easton Neston	N	SGL		Towcester Ironworks	
			NGL		E&WJR Ravenstonewood Jc-Towcester	1920
1873	Hunsbury Hill	N	NGH		Hunsbury Ironworks	1921
			NGL		Hunsbury Ironworks	
1873	Spratton	N	NGL	I?	LNWR Northampton-Market Harborough	1911(a)
1873	Brixworth (A&T/Clay Cross)	N	NGL		LNWR Northampton-Market Harborough	1947
1873	Ditchford (Whitehouse)	N	NG		LNWR Blisworth-Peterborough	1885
1873	Ringstead (Newbridge)	N	NG		LNWR Blisworth-Peterborough	1882
1873	Thrapston	N	NG		MR Kettering-Cambridge	1887
1873	Desborough (Stanton)	N	NG	I	MR Bedford-Leicester	c.1899
1873	Desborough (Ball)	N	NG or Rd.		MR Bedford-Leicester	1875

Year of Opening	Name of Quarry	County	Transport System	Special F'tures	Main Line Connection or Terminus	Year of Closure
1873	Desborough (Wells/Wheldon)	N	SG		MR Bedford-Leicester	1882
1873	Burton Latimer	N	SG		MR Kettering-Cambridge	1921
1873	Cransley	N	NGL		MR Kettering-Cambridge	1891
1873	Easton on the Hill	N	NGL		Cransley Ironworks	
			NG	I.	MR Melton Mowbray-Peterborough	
			Rd.		MR Melton Mowbray-Peterborough	
			NGL	I	MR Melton Mowbray-Peterborough	c.1919
1873	Monks Abbey	Li	NGH	I.M	MSLR Lincoln-Barnetby	c.1881
1873	Greetwell	Li	NGH	M	MSLR Lincoln-Barnetby	
			NGL		MSLR Lincoln-Barnetby	1939
1874	Wellingborough (Rixon)	N	NGL	M	MR Bedford-Leicester	1966
1874	Coleby	Li	NG	M	GNR Grantham-Lincoln	c.1876
1875	Cranford West	N	NGH		MR Kettering-Cambridge	
			NGL		MR Kettering-Cambridge	
			NGC	M	MR Kettering-Cambridge	1926
1875	Stantongate	N	NG/SG	M	MR Bedford-Leicester	c.1895
1875	Finedonhill	N	NGC	I.M	MR Bedford-Leicester	1918
1875	Ditchford (Rixon)	N	NG		LNWR Blisworth-Peterborough	1881
1875	Holwell (Holwell)	Le	NG/SGL		MR Melton Mowbray-Nottingham	
			NG	I?	MR Holwell Branch	1890

Year of Opening	Name of Quarry	County	Transport System	Special F'tures	Main Line Connection or Terminus	Year of Closure
c.1875	Irchester	N	NGL		LNWR Blisworth-Peterborough	
			SGL		LNWR Blisworth-Peterborough	1969
1877	Addington (Walters)	N	SGL		LNWR Blisworth-Peterborough	1895
1878	Desborough (Smith)	N	NG	I	MR Bedford-Leicester	1884
1879	Holwell (Stanton)	Le	NGH		MR Holwell Branch	
			NGL	I.M	MR Holwell Branch	
			Rd.		BR Holwell Branch	1962
1879	Wartnaby	Le	NGL	I	MR Melton Mowbray-Nottingham	1929
1880	Corby (Lloyds)	N	SGL		MR Kettering-Manton	
			SGL		Corby Ironworks	1980
1880	Thingdon	N	NGC	I.M	MR Bedford-Leicester	1911
1880	Tilton	Le	SGH	I	LNWR/GNR Joint Northampton-Melton Mowbray	
			NGH		LNWR/GNR Joint Northampton-Melton Mowbray	
			NGL		LMSR/LNER Joint Northampton-Melton Mowbray	
			Rd.		BR Northampton-Melton Mowbray	1961
c.1880	Caythorpe Town (Cohen)	Li	SGML		GNR Grantham-Lincoln	c.1906
c.1880	Caythorpe Station (West Yorks)	Li	SGML		GNR Grantham-Lincoln	c.1897
c.1880	Caythorpe (West Yorks)	Li	SGML		GNR Grantham-Lincoln	c.1912

Year of Opening	Name of Quarry	County	Transport System	Special F'tures	Main Line Connection or Terminus	Year of Closure
1881	Raunds	N	SGL		MR Kettering-Cambridge	1882
1881	Eastwell	Le	NGL	I	LNWR/GNR Joint Melton Mowbray-Bottesford	
			Rd.		BR Melton Mowbray-Bottesford	1967
1882	Lamport (Glendon)	N	SGL		LNWR Northampton-Market Harborough	1890
1882	Desborough (Sheepbridge)	N	NGH		MR Bedford-Leicester	
			SGL		MR Bedford-Leicester	
			SGL+Rd.		BR Bedford-Leicester	1966
1882	Desborough (Pain)	N	Rd.		MR Bedford-Leicester	1884
1882	Waltham-on-the-Wolds (Waltham)	Le	NG		GNR Waltham-on-the-Wolds Branch	1885
1882	Cottesmore	R	NGH	I	MR Cottesmore Branch	
			NGL	I	MR Cottesmore Branch	
			Rd.		BR Cottesmore Branch	1964
1883	Barton Seagrave	N	NG/SG		MR Kettering-Cambridge	c.1891
1883	Wartnaby (Blenkinsop)	Le	NG		MR Melton Mowbray-Nottingham?	c.1896
1883	Waltham-on-the-Wolds (Holwell)	Le	NGL		GNR Waltham-on-the-Wolds Branch	1885
1883	Woolsthorpe	Le/Li	NGL	I	GNR Denton Branch	
					GNR Denton Branch	
			SGL+Rd.		BR Denton Branch	1974
1884	Brixworth (Sheepbridge)	N	NG?	I?	LNWR Northampton-Market Harborough	1896

Year of Opening	Name of Quarry	County	Transport System	Special F'tures	Main Line Connection or Terminus	Year of Closure
1884	Cliff Road	Li	SGML		GNR Grantham-Lincoln	1896
1885	Denford (Glendon)	N	NG		LNWR Blisworth-Peterborough	1885?
1885	Cranford (Butlins)	N	NG?		MR Kettering-Cambridge	1891
1885	Eaton	Le	NGL/AeR		GNR Eaton Branch	
			SGL		GNR Eaton Branch	
			Rd		BR Eaton Branch	1962
1885	Waltham (Waltham)	Le	NGL		GNR Eaton Branch	1958
1885	Holwell (Davies)	Le	NGH?		MR Holwell Branch	1908
1886	Corby (Pain)	N	SGL		MR Kettering-Manton	1912
c.1887	Caythorpe Station (Cohen/Burke)	Li	SGML		GNR Grantham-Lincoln	c.1902
1888	Gretton	N	NGL		MR Kettering-Manton	1902
1889	Hook Norton (HNIP)	O	NGL/SGL	I	GWR Kings Sutton-Chipping Norton	c.1901
1890	Irthlingborough (IIO)	N	SGL		LNWR Blisworth-Peterborough	1898
c.1890	Adderbury (HNIP)	O	NGL		GWR Kings Sutton-Chipping Norton	
			NGH	I	GWR Kings Sutton-Chipping Norton	c.1929
1891	Chelveston	N	NGH?/Rd		Wellingborough Ironworks	1892
1891	Great Addington (Butlins)	N	NG/SG		LNWR Blisworth-Peterborough	1892
1891	Loddington	N	NGL		MR Loddington Branch	
			SGL		BR Loddington Branch	1963

Year of Opening	Name of Quarry	County	Transport System	Special F'tures	Main Line Connection or Terminus	Year of Closure
c.1891	Hook Norton (Baker)	O	Rd.		GWR Kings Sutton-Chipping Norton	c.1918
1892	Ab Kettleby	Le	NGL		MR Holwell Branch	1907
c.1892	Carlton Scroop	Li	NG		GNR Grantham-Lincoln	1897
1893	Irchester (Stanton)	N	Rd.		MR Higham Ferrers Branch	1908
1895	West End	N	SGL		LNWR Blisworth-Peterborough	1906
1896	Great Tew	O	Rd.		GWR Kings Sutton-Chipping Norton?	1900
c.1896	Leadenham	Li	NG		GNR Grantham-Lincoln	1925
1897	Astrop	N	NGC	K	GWR Oxford-Leamington	1924
c.1897	Geddington	N	NGL		MR Kettering-Manton	
	Storefield		SGL		LMSR Kettering-Manton	1971
c.1897	Fulbeck South	Li	SGML		GNR Grantham-Lincoln	c.1906
c.1897	The Ings	Li	SGML		GNR Grantham-Lincoln	c.1902
1898	Cranford East	N	NGL	I	MR Kettering-Cambridge	
			SGL		LMSR Kettering-Cambridge	1969
1898	Rothwell Hill	N	NGC/L Rd/AeR	I	MR Bedford-Leicester Corby Ironworks	1966
1898	Buckminster	Li/Le	SGL+Rd.		MR Saxby-Bourne	1973
c.1898	Heath	Li	SGML		GNR Grantham-Lincoln	c.1900
1899	Blisworth (Phipps)	N	NGH		Grand Junction Canal	c.1912
1899	Hook Norton (Brymbo)	O	NGL	K	GWR Kings Sutton-Chipping Norton	1947
1900	Isham	N	SGL		MR Bedford-Leicester	1911

Year of Opening	Name of Quarry	County	Transport System	Special F'tures	Main Line Connection or Terminus	Year of Closure
1901	Midland Brick	N	NG		MR Bedford-Leicester	1940
			Rd.		Wellingborough Ironworks	
1901	Hook Norton (Earl of Dudley)	O	NGC		GWR Kings Sutton-Chipping Norton	1916
1902	Orton	N	NGC/L	I	LNWR Northampton-Market Harborough	1921
1902	Honington	Li	SGML/NG	I	GNR Grantham-Lincoln	1921
			SGML		GNR Grantham-Lincoln	
c.1902	Frieston	Li	SGL		GNR Grantham-Lincoln	1946
1905	Desborough (Co-Op)	N	SGL/NGH		MR Bedford-Leicester	1926
			SGL/NGL		LMSR Bedford-Leicester	
1906	Twywell	N	NGC		MR Kettering-Cambridge	1969
			Rd.		BR Kettering-Cambridge	
1906	Market Overton	R	SGL		MR Saxby-Bourne	1971
			SGL		BR High Dyke	
1908	Fulbeck	Li	SGML		GNR Grantham-Lincoln	1930
1909	Showsley	N	NGH?		SMJ Towcester-Olney	1918
1913	Lamport (Staveley)	N	NGL/AeR		LNWR Northampton-Market Harborough	1963
			SGL		LMSR Northampton-Market Harborough	
1913	Finedon Park	N	SGL/NGL		MR Bedford-Leicester	1921
1913	Ditchford (Ward)	N	NG	I?	LNWR Blisworth-Peterborough	1918
1913	Denford (Keeble)	N	NG		LNWR Blisworth-Peterborough	c.1917
1913	Wakerley	N	NGH/NGL	K	LNWR Rugby-Peterborough	1921

Year of Opening	Name of Quarry	County	Transport System	Special F'tures	Main Line Connection or Terminus	Year of Closure
1914	Whiston	N	SGL		LNWR Blisworth-Peterborough	c.1920
1914	Uppingham	R	SGL		LNWR Uppingham Branch	1926
1915	Earls Barton	N	NGL/AeR		LNWR Blisworth-Peterborough	1921
1916	Eaton Basic	Le	Rd.		GNR Eaton Branch	1965
1917	Byfield	N	SGL		SMJ Woodford-Fenny Compton	1965
1917	Charwelton	N	SGL		GCR Woodford-Leicester	1961
1917	Sydenham	O	NGL		GWR Kings Sutton-Chipping Norton	1925
1917	Colsterworth	Li	SGL+Rd	K	GNR High Dyke Branch	1973
1918	Bloxham (B&W)	O	SGL		GWR Kings Sutton-Chipping Norton	1927
1918	Bloxham (Clay Cross)	O	SGL		GWR Kings Sutton-Chipping Norton	1954
1919	Luffenham	R	SGL/NGL		MR Melton Mowbray-Peterborough	1925
1919	Pilton	R	SGL		MR Melton Mowbray-Peterborough	1969
1919	Wroxton	O	SGL		GWR Oxford-Leamington	1967
1920	South Hill	N	NGL		MR Bedford-Leicester	c.1924
1920	Irthlingborough (EV)	N	NGL/SGL	K M	LNWR Blisworth-Peterborough	1965
1920	Burley	R	NGL/SGL		MR Cottesmore Branch	
			SGL		LMSR Cottesmore Branch	1962
1922	Edge Hill	W	SGL	I	SMJ Fenny Compton-Stratford	1925
1924	Harringworth	N	NGL		LMSR Kettering-Manton	
			SGL		LMSR Kettering-Manton	
			SGL		Corby Ironworks	1980

Year of Opening	Name of Quarry	County	Transport System	Special F'tures	Main Line Connection or Terminus	Year of Closure
1925	Pitsford	N	SGL/NGL		LMSR Northampton-Market Harborough	1965
1925	Sproxton	Le	SGH		LNER High Dyke Branch	
			SGL		LNER High Dyke Branch	
1930	Nettleton	Li	Rd.		BR High Dyke Branch	1973
			NGL/AeR	M	LNER Lincoln-Barnetby	
			NGL/Rd.	M	BR Lincoln-Barnetby	1968
1936	Cringle	Li	SGL		LNER High Dyke Branch	1958
1939	Nassington	N	SGL		LMSR Rugby-Peterborough	1970
1941	Harlaxton	Li	SGL		LNER Denton Branch	
			Rd		BR Denton Branch	1977
1942	Blisworth (RTB)	N	SGL		LMSR Blisworth-Towcester	1967
1942	Barrowden	R	Rd.		LMSR Rugby-Peterborough	1948
1944	Thistleton	R	NGL/SGL	M	LNER High Dyke Branch	1964
c.1950	Wansford	N	Rd.		BR Rugby-Peterborough	1967
1951	Exton Park	R	SGL		BR Cottesmore Branch	1973
1952	Rushton	N	Rd.		BR Bedford-Leicester	1967
1957	Mill Hill	Le	SGL		BR Eaton Branch	
			Rd.		BR Eaton Branch	1967
1958	Easton	Li	NGC/SGL	M	BR High Dyke Branch	1967

(a) Quarries reopened 1939-44 as part of Lamport system

INDEX

Index